Mister Jolson
And all that Jazz

Stan Henderson

Published in 2020 by Stan Henderson

© Copyright Stan Henderson

ISBN: 978-1-913898-04-5

Book & Cover Design by Russell Holden

Pixel Tweaks Publications
SELF-PUBLISHING MADE SIMPLE

www.pixeltweakspublications.com

A Catalogue record for this book is available from the British Library.

Printed by Ingram

All rights reserved without limiting the rights under copyright reserved above, no parts of this publication may be reproduced, stored in or introduced into a retrieval system, or transmitted in any form, or by any means (electronic, mechanical, photocopying, recording or otherwise) without the prior written permission of both the copyright owner and the publisher of this book.

You Ain't Heard Nothin' Yet!

The famous Jolson exhortation, with its double-negative, was almost as well-known as some of the sayings of Winston Churchill. First heard by people outside of the USA in the 1927 picture – *The Jazz Singer,* which is an actual American cultural classic. According to biographer, Michael Freedland, Jolson first uttered this in San Francisco in the aftermath of the 1906 earthquake. In his book, *Tenor: History of a voice,* author and singer, John Potter tells us that Jolson first used the saying in 1918 at the Century theatre in New York City during a benefit show for First World War veterans. (*When Jolson voiced his cri-de-coeur in The Jazz Singer, he obviously did not realise just how prophetic he was being*).

CONTENTS

INTRODUCTION

COPYRIGHT

PREFACE & ACKNOWLEDGEMENTS

CHAPTER ONE 1

CHAPTER TWO 7

CHAPTER THREE 17

CHAPTER FOUR 21

CHAPTER FIVE 29

CHAPTER SIX 35

CHAPTER SEVEN 41

EPILOGUE 49

APPENDIX 55

INDEX 68

INTRODUCTION

This work is what could be described as a *Coffee Table Book*. It is a kind of sanitized, part-biography, and is not offered as a serious reference work or *exposé*. It is also a celebration of the *popular art* and one man's way of giving something back to a musical genre that almost disappeared around 1955. The genre referred to was the mainstream before the advent of Rock and Roll and has since become known as The Great American Song Book, a canon, being a collection of American popular songs and jazz standards. Who would have ever thought that such as *Tutti Frutti* would have supplanted gems like *Stardust, It Had to Be You*, or *All the Things You Are?*

When considering the canon, names like Harold Arlen; Irving Berlin; Dorothy Fields; George and Ira Gershwin; Jerome Kern; Louis Armstrong; Ethel Waters; Bing Crosby; Frank Sinatra and Al Jolson come to mind. This book concerns itself mainly with the career of the latter during 1916 to 1931, also his influence on the development of popular singing *via* the Afro-American idiom.

"His way with the idiom would influence just about every popular singer who came after him, male and female, black and white", Henry Pleasants, (Ref.2).

The tapestry of Jolson's life is complex, colourful, and eventful, being far beyond the scope of this book. And, as entertaining as they were, the two films about his life fell short in conveying this. Anyone wishing to learn more about the private Jolson or his later career, is therefore referred to the excellent work of Herbert G. Goldman, (Ref.1).

There is a school of thought that speaks of jazz as being inherent in the make-up of the black race – being encoded in their genes. *They certainly appear to have innate rhythm in their bones.* Jazz was without doubt devised by blacks as a rebellion against white orchestral music, and has been evolving since the dawn of the 20th century. The hot jazz of the Roaring Twenties with its two-beat style gave way to a more sophisticated, four-beat, interpretation – becoming almost 'polite'.

"I heard some music tonight, something they call. . . Jazz"- The Jolson Story.
During the period under review there was no equivalent of today's mass popular music (popular culture transitioned into mass culture). Also nothing like today's classical. So please join me on an excursion into the past to see what all the excitement was about.

COPYRIGHT

This book relies very heavily indeed on references to, and quotations from, numerous publications and I have of necessity taken advantage of such latitude as is allowed by Copyright Law and common practice to take short quotations without specific permission, for the purpose of 'fair comment and review'. I have, however, included a comprehensive Bibliography of the works referenced herein. I would like to express my appreciation to the authors and owners of the copyright involved, and indeed to all those whose writings on the subjects discussed have given me such pleasure and stimulation over the years.

Notwithstanding the foregoing, permission is pending for the use of extracts and quotes from references, (1) and (2).

Many of the Jolson related photographs in circulation, including some used herein, emanated (circa 1981) from the office of the late Otis R. Lowe when he was the Photo Department Director of the International Jolson Society.

Permission has been sought from the Shubert Organisation for use of the image of *Jolson's 59th street Theatre* (p.18).

Other images used are sourced from the public domain under Creative Commons licensing.

PREFACE & ACKNOWLEDGEMENTS

In 1955 my grandmother was having a clear-out at her home. Many of the things being discarded belonged to her late husband – my grandfather – who had passed away in 1951. One of the items destined for the tip was an old wind-up gramophone and a collection of 78-rpm records, which I had shown interest in many times in the past when visiting her home. I asked my mother if we could take possession of the *'relic'*, as gran would refer to it, and the upshot was that it ended-up in our parlour. This room, that housed my sister's upright piano and only accustomed to *Bach fugues*, was to vibrate to a totally different idiom! My grandmother's rubbish heap would become my gold mine.

Among the records, which comprised mainly of 1930s dance-band stuff, were several recordings by G.H.Elliot, aka *the chocolate-coloured coon*, including - *Lilly of Laguna; Sue* and *I Used to Sigh for the Silvery Moon. Keep Your Sunny Side Up* (Johnny Hamp); Denny Dennis with Ambrose; several jazz standards e.g. *Running Wild* and also a half dozen Al Jolson records, viz: *My Mammy, Sonny Boy, Waiting for the Robert E. Lee* and one that I particularly liked – *My Mother's Rosary*. Working my way through all these recordings I always found myself returning to the Jolson discs. Not because I found the songs to have any particular artistic merit nor indeed any sophistication, but because something in that unusual, *leathery,* bass-baritone just communicated itself to me. Was it the tonal quality (timbre)? Whatever it was it was different, in several ways, to anything I had heard before. It was a voice that enchanted my ear.

Such was my introduction to the singer who, throughout my early life, was responsible for more than a few missing homework papers – especially when his biographical films were airing on television. From 1964 and after I had left school, Al took a back seat for a while as I became enamoured of the burgeoning 1960s pop scene. Then, from the early 1970s, as my musical tastes began to mature, I found myself tuning into BBC Radio 2 and listening to what presenters like the late David Jacobs and Hubert Gregg called 'Our Kind of Music' (Mr Sinatra referred to it as *'Polite Jazz'*). I discovered such as Cole Porter, Dubin and Warren; Rodgers and Hart.

Being an inquisitive person, I started to delve into the life and career of the man. I somehow felt the need to justify my fascination in this performer who had constantly referred to himself as the *World's Greatest Entertainer.*[*] Interestingly, during his lifetime, no one argued with this claim but to me, having seen only a couple of his early films, the billing seemed preposterous. Following his death, while many still held the view that he was *the greatest*, there were those who dismissed him as an embarrassing ham. Nevertheless I decided to continue researching his life while keeping both viewpoints in mind. My starting point was a letter to Larry Adler (1979), who had seen Al work on Broadway. He replied thus: *"As good as he was in films, and The Jazz Singer saved Warner Bros., you had to see the man before a live audience. I would bet that none of his present-day detractors had this experience".*

In 1976, after having read Michael Freedland's 1972 book – *Jolson* – I joined the International Al Jolson Society. This is possibly the world's oldest fan club having been formed in 1950 after the singer's death when the original club – The Jolsonaires – who had formed some years earlier, for some reason, disbanded. Run from the USA it has chapters in many countries around the globe. Around 1980 I began writing articles for the *Jolson Journal*

---

* Contrary to what has been written, Jolson did not brand himself The World's Greatest Entertainer. This was a commercial contrivance of the Schubert brothers who were simply capitalising on the popularity of their 'Winter Garden Nightingale'.

and then about two years later I also contributed stories to *Perfectly Frank* which is the magazine of the Sinatra Music Society. It was *via* the latter that I made some good media contacts. The highest profile celebrity member of the Jolson Society was the late singer, Frankie Laine (*Mr Rhythm*) who was an avid fan. He would always reply to my letters and requests for information, and was a true gentleman.

Apropos 'the world's greatest entertainer' claim, some have cited the jazz dancer, James Barton also Sammy Davies Jnr as being more befitting of the title. (Davies was certainly more versatile). However, Jolson qualifies in that, without any mechanical gadgets *i.e.* musical instruments, microphones or indeed any props, just by the sheer force of his artistry, personality and God-given talent, during the first quarter of the 20th century, he brought the whole world to its feet. No one, according to Herb Goldman, has come closer to giving audiences the genuine experience that Al Jolson did. In this sense alone, he lived up to his billing.

In his book *Call Them Irreplaceable,* John Fisher states that "No other performer came closer to embodying the concept of the performer as a force of nature".

To illustrate what Fisher is trying to convey, I remember what Ralph Reader, one of several celebrity correspondents of mine, told me when I was writing for fan club magazines in the early 1980s. Reader was attempting to explain the Jolson phenomenon to a group of young people: "It wasn't that he wanted to give so much", he said, "It was that he **had** to".

One of the amazing things I first discovered was that Jolson's phenomenal popularity, in the two separate professional phases of his life, was due, in part, to others! Whereas his comeback after World War II was largely down to the non-singing actor, Larry Parks (who invented a more modern Jolson shtick). His initial rise to fame was courtesy of a harlequin-type, fictional character called Gus Jackson (the Winter Garden muse).

Gus was the underdog who lived by his wits, he was a man of many parts, his wit and bathos were singularly peculiar to Gus and not Jolson [a hint at the duality of human nature?]. Critic Gilbert Seldes, who saw all of Jolson's shows, insists that Al actually became this black character, this alter ego, when on stage.

The main reference sources for this book are *JOLSON: The Legend Comes to Life* by Herbert G. Goldman, which is the definitive biography, and also The Great American Popular Singers by Henry Pleasants. They are quoted and paraphrased substantively in the text.

Thanks are extended to all the celebrity correspondents who took the trouble to answer my questions and reply to my letters. To Glenys Day and the late Charlie Hackett of the Sinatra Music Society and also to colleagues in the International Al Jolson Society who, over many years, helped with source material, photos, encouragement etc. They are: Stan Ball; Sheila Biesold; Terry Brule; Stan Gerloff; Jim Harris; Leslie Kaye; Marc I. Leavey, M.D., David Mc Carthy and Terry Owen.

Stan Henderson
Kirkby-in-Furness, 2020.

*This book is dedicated to the memory of
Michael Freedland and Benny Green.*

CHAPTER ONE

Sometime around the end of the 19th Century there had been a gradual migration from Europe to the *New World*. Thousands of people crossed the Atlantic Ocean and settled on the eastern seaboard of the USA. Many of these immigrants brought creative talents, also divers languages, such as Yiddish, Italian, German, Irish, Scottish and Welsh with them. This *Cultural Revolution* resulted in the emergence of the subject idiom and what we now know as The Great American Songbook – *a canon* – representing the most influential American standard songs. It came, first, out of Tin Pan Alley, and then later from Hollywood when words and music were needed for the new talking pictures phenomenon. Familiar names, such as Gershwin, Berlin, Cohan, Harrigan, Kelly and later Yoelson appeared. Some came to escape persecution and poverty in their own country and some just in search of a better life. The streets of America weren't paved with gold, but they were at least paved.

Our story begins in 1916 New York where a 30-years old Russian-Jewish émigré, Al Jolson – billed as America's greatest entertainer – was approaching the pinnacle of his career. Between 1911 and 1931 Al Jolson starred in about ten sell-out Broadway shows. (Probably some of the weakest shows in the history of The Great White Way). In these musicals he was always in blackface and usually playing the same role – Gus Jackson – a valet, chauffeur or waiter. *(Prior to Jolson, blackface had not been seen in the legitimate theatre)*.[1]

In 1916 Al Jolson was on the crest of a wave. Working for the Shubert Brothers, theatre owners, and impresarios, he was pulling down around $10,000 per week. He had been at the New York Winter Garden since its opening in 1911, co-starring with the likes of buxom comedienne Stella Mayhew and the internationally acclaimed Mme Gaby DesLys. Mae West and Fanny Brice also made fleeting appearances.

Working with Jolson around this time had been dancer and cross-dresser, Kitty Doner. Had things been different, Kitty could have become Mrs Jolson. Al had been a married man since 1907 but kept telling Kitty that he would soon be getting divorced.[2] Kitty and Al shared a strange relationship in that they worked together professionally – almost becoming a double act. They would also display a tenderness towards each other, exchanging gifts and sharing days out but on some occasions Jolson would not even acknowledge her existence. Kitty Doner, born Catherine Donohue in Chicago of English parents, was considered the best male impersonator in America, comparing favourably with Britain's Vesta Tilley. Kitty and Jolson finally parted company in 1919.

The Winter Garden Theatre, located at 1634 Broadway between 50th and 51st streets, occupied the same footprint as the old Horse Exchange building. The conversion took place during 1910 -11 and the space made available by the partial demolition of the Horse Exchange dictated that the architects design a playhouse that was unusually wide. In fact, the proscenium opening is still the widest of all the Shubert theatres. Despite the steel roof trusses of the former being left exposed, architect William Swasey gave the theatre a lavish interior with a sky-blue ceiling, complete with a floral centrepiece (garden motif). The entire auditorium was latticed and carpeted and very spacious. There was a blue Dutch café and wine bar on the mezzanine and the box fronts were adorned with garlands and leaves. The lavish new theatre opened on 10 March 1911 and for the first ten years of its operation it had a runway* into the audience. This was dubbed by audiences as "The Bridge of Thighs". Due to the size of its auditorium, stage and backstage facilities, it is a house favoured by sponsors of large musical productions (seating capacity: 1526).

The Author on 59th Street, New York City, directly opposite the Plaza Hotel, 1989. S. Henderson

In 1989, while on a study tour in New York City, I went to see Cats *at the Winter Garden.* Cats *was the theatre's longest-staying tenant, running for almost eighteen years and although the auditorium and stage had been drastically modified for the show, parts of the Horse Exchange's trusses, to the rear of the auditorium, were still visible. When* Cats *closed in 2001 the theatre underwent a multi-million dollar restoration to its former 20s glory.*

---

* Contrary to what we were told in *The Jolson Story* (1946); the runway was not a Jolson innovation, although he did make good use of it.

The Winter Garden façade, Broadway, 1989. S. Henderson

Jolson biographer Herb Goldman tells us that: The medium (blackface), allowed him to show pluck and daring – an élan visible in the harlequin but also traceable in the black man's cultural approach to entertainment, sports and striking back, where possible, at white society and the subservient role it forced him to assume. In time the black faced Jolson would display an élan on the Broadway stage that no other performer – black or white – would dare exhibit. There was a magic to his work in blackface that he never captured sans the burnt cork. Ref.1.

The Winter Garden show of 1916 was *Robinson Crusoe Jr* - described as a piece of nonsense in two acts and ten scenes. The plot involved itself with a millionaire (Mr Poindexter) who falls asleep and dreams that he is Robinson Crusoe. During his reverie a film-making company moves onto his estate to make a picture. Poindexter's chauffeur, Gus Jackson (Jolson), became Man Friday. *Jolson was seldom the protagonist in any of these shows. This allowed him the latitude to always 'save his master's bacon'. As Gus the chauffeur, plantation slave or even gondolier, his scheming, and quick thinking always saved the day.* In the audience for one of the performances was playwright Samson Raphaelson, who would soon write a short story based on Jolson's life, called *Day of Atonement*. It would later become the basis for The Jazz Singer. Witnessing Jolson vocalising, he proclaimed: "My God, this isn't a jazz singer, this is a cantor!" *Years later Raphaelson told Al that seeing Robinson*

Crusoe Jr. gave him the inspiration for Day of Atonement. "Hell, I loved to see those shows", he said. "But I wouldn't be caught dead writing one!"

On 15th August, 1916 the show started a 15-month national tour at the Nixon Apollo theatre in Atlantic City. Shortly after the following testimonial appeared in the Morning Telegraph – *"I happened to be in Boston last Saturday and in the evening went to see Al Jolson in Robinson Crusoe Jr. When this production was in New York, at the Winter Garden, I saw it several times, and always enjoyed it; but in all my experience as a theatre-goer, I had never seen a performer receive such an ovation as Mr Jolson did last Saturday evening.*

Jolson has made his audiences laugh and applaud at the Winter Garden and other places, but at the Shubert theatre in Boston the audience yelled. In fact, I have never heard such cheering and such enthusiasm given to a performer or to a performance in all my experience as a theatre-goer, which covers a period of over 20-years. Mr Jolson had to plead with his audience. Some of the audience stood up, cheered, applauded, and threw hats in the air simultaneously during the second act. To be exact Mr Jolson stopped the show three times, and in each instance a scene was delayed and the audience simply wouldn't allow the performance to proceed".

During one of the performances, Al interpolated that song written by James V. Monaco and Joe McCarthy, *You Made Me Love You (I Didn't Want to Do it)*, which he had recorded in June, 1913. In doing so he renewed the implicit social contract between performer and listener and the number went on to become a standard.[3] More than twenty years later, a 14 years-old Judy Garland would sing it as a hymn to her screen idol, Clark Gable, in the film *Broadway Melody of 1938*. Other notable songs in Robinson Crusoe Jr. were, *Down Where the Swanee River flows; Now He's got a Beautiful Girl; Yaaka Hula Hickey Dula* and *Where Did Robinson Crusoe Go with Friday on Saturday Night?*

Kitty Doner had been Al's constant companion throughout the run of the show, always referring to him as *Mister*. Years later, when asked to reminisce about her time with him, she would always say, "No one funnier than *Mister*". Robinson Crusoe Jr. closed in November, 1917.

Kitty Doner.
Kitty and Al appeared in three Extravaganzas together.

Green Book Magazine (September 1916) Public Domain

Notes to Chapter One:

1. The term Legitimate Theatre speaks almost of a kind of class distinction between the two types of premises. It dates back to the Licensing Act of 1737 where licensed (privileged houses) could show serious 'spoken' drama. The illegitimate houses, such as music halls and burlesque theatres, could show/sell such as comedy, pantomime and general musical entertainment. The Act was finally suspended in 1968

2. In June 1919, Jolson's first wife, Henrietta, sued for divorce.

3. Jolson first introduced the number in the show: Honeymoon Express (1913).

CHAPTER TWO

In 1918 if you wanted to hear Jolson (or even operatic tenor Enrico Caruso) sing you had to be where they were – or own a Victrola phonograph. In 1918 Caruso and Jolson were the most successful singers on the planet and although poles apart i.e. classical v 'pop' they had more in common than, say, Placido Domingo and Sting. In the days before microphones and amplification, exponents of both codes had to sing in a full-throated and somewhat stilted, stylised way. To project their voices a long way they had to sing with their larynxes lower than in normal speech. This maximised their acoustic efficiency and as a by-product gave them the richer sound that we now associate with classical singers.[1] As a singer in the first quarter of the 20th century, you had to make yourself heard by those on the back row of the gallery. Crooning, with its subtle nuances and conversational style, was still in the future. Before Jolson there were no pop singers as such. The mainstream consisted of pompous platform tenors and bumptious baritones who would anchor themselves in the bend of the piano. Al Jolson bridged the gap between the stage and the stalls. In stripping off his tie, opening his shirt front and addressing the audience direct he was, according to some critics, compounding the impudence of boorish behaviour. To them, performers should treat the paying public with deference, not address them as 'folks'. Years later, when the likes of Sinatra, Dean Martin or Tom Jones did this, their fans believed the practice had started with them.

Al Jolson in 1918   Enrico Caruso in 1918
both images, S. Henderson collection

The year 1918 saw the end of the Great War. On Sunday, September 15th the mammoth Century Theatre in midtown Manhattan was host to a special programme sponsored by the U.S. Army Tank Corps Welfare League. George M. Cohan (the original Yankee Doodle Dandy), who had just penned his famous song *Over There,* was on the bill, also Sam Bernard, William Colyer and Sig. Caruso. The maestro had sung two songs in Italian from his repertoire, finishing with a rousing rendition of *Over There* – to the rapturous applause of the audience. Before applause for the world's greatest tenor had died down, onto the stage bounced Jolson who made with a shrill whistle followed by, *"Wait a minute folks, you ain't heard nothing yet!"* The audience went wild, they wouldn't let him leave the stage. *Seventy three years later the event was related by the Jewish comedian George Burns [who was in that audience] to Johnny Carson (Carson Tonight, November 10, 1989). It may still be available on YouTube.*

After the show Caruso took Jolson back to his hotel where he invited the 'jazz singer' to duet with him at the Met. Jolson declined the offer, suggesting the opera critics would go daffy! The pairing was not to be but Jolson, being aware that opera was of sufficient high status to make it worth satirising, as in his hilarious (at the time) Pagliacci sketch, would continue with his burlesque of the genre.

Jolson's next show at the Winter Garden was *Sinbad*, another extravaganza similar to *Robinson Crusoe Jr*, which opened on February 14th 1918. The two-act extravaganza had Al singing in flashback roles as Sinbad the Sailor, as the familiar Gus and also the front end of a speaking mule (Emil). The show is memorable because it contained three of his most famous songs, *viz.* Rock-a-Bye; Swanee and My *Mammy*.

Jolson, at the time, was still being classed as a singing comedian. However, his first number in the show was Rock-a-bye. Charles Darnton, writing in *The World*, noted – *"Whether he knows it or not, Jolson hit the singing mark of his career with Rock-a-bye Your Baby with a Dixie Melody". He sang the first chorus over the heads of the audience, as if he were alone in a vast theatre. On the second chorus he seemed to reach out, yearning for them to embrace him. The power of that yearning, coupled with the snugly rhyming couplets of the lyric, ensured the song would bid fair to become a standard".*

The other songs were *Why Do They All Take the Night Boat to Albany?; Cleopatra; I Wonder Why She Kept On Saying, Si, Si, Si Senor;* and *N' Everything.* Critic Gilbert Seldes, singled out the latter for his essay on Jolson – *In the first weeks of Sinbad, he sang the words of N' Everything as they are printed. Gradually (I saw the show in many phases), he interpolated, improvised, always with his absolute sense of rhythmic effect; until at the end it was a series of amorous cries and shouts of triumph to* Eros. It was during *Sinbad's* run that Jolson decided his name should appear as co-writer on some of the numbers he interpolated into his shows. The practice became known as a 'cut-in' and no fewer than five of the published songs from *Sinbad* had his name among the writer's credits. Song writers and pluggers now actively courted Al, hoping he would introduce their efforts into his shows.

Sheet music for Si Si Si Si Si Senor: Courtesy of the International Al Jolson Society, JJ.132

Chapter Two

During its run *Sinbad* opened and closed twice because Al decided he needed to take things easy. It was common knowledge among his colleagues that he was something of a hypochondriac, with a morbid interest in medical matters (perhaps not in the same league as Proust, but equally preoccupied). He would go all through his life with a fear of losing his voice and worse still, the dread of contracting tuberculosis. As a kind of insurance premium he agreed to donate the royalties from the aforementioned songs to the sanatorium at Saranac Lake, New York. *(Scottish author, Robert Louis Stevenson had stayed there in 1887).*

The following year *Sinbad* had a very profitable run at the Boston Opera House. In addition, Al gave a recital there on Sunday 18 May, 1919 accompanied by the 50-piece Boston Symphony Orchestra under the baton of his own conductor, Al Goodman. It was the first time in history that an entertainer had given his own *soirée* at an opera house. During the evening he performed 17 of his favourite songs. More than $4,000 were taken and around 1800 people had to be turned away.

Later in 1919, when *Sinbad* was playing in Hartford, Connecticut, Al was to make the acquaintance of the singer-song writing duo, Noble Sissle and Eubie Blake (a few years later they would pen the song, I'm Just Wild about Harry). Sissle's early career was spent largely in vaudeville as a singer. However, his talents as a songwriter gradually drew him to Broadway where, in collaboration with Eubie Blake, he achieved a major breakthrough. Before Sissle and Blake it was rare for a black entertainer to gain acceptance on the *Great White Way*, but the success of their 1921 show, *Shuffle Along*, as well as Jolson's persistence, changed all that. The show brought authentic black artistry to the American stage. "After we did our first show", Sissle told Martin Abramson shortly after Jolson's death, "we went into a dirty little restaurant to get a bite to eat, the owner took one look at us and told us to get the hell out as we don't serve coloureds. Outside we bumped into a reporter from a local paper and told him about the incident. Sure enough the next day the paper featured an item about our experience. To our amazement we promptly got a call from Al Jolson, who happened to be in town and although we were two unimportant guys whom he'd never heard of until that morning, he was so annoyed about the story that he wanted to make it up to us. Well, that night he came over in a big car and said he was taking us to the swellest restaurant in town and he'd punch anyone who tried to kick us out. I can't tell you how grateful we were to him, but we told him we didn't like to go anywhere we weren't wanted. Then Jolson said, wait a minute, I know where we can have a good time! He turned the car around, drove us to a Jewish deli and treated us to a wonderful meal. Then he bought a load of pastrami sandwiches and took them out to the car. We sat in his car until the early hours of the morning eating our heads off and listening to the greatest star in America performing, just for us". They remained friends thereafter. (In 1950 Sissle was president of the Black Actors Guild and represented that organisation at Al's funeral).

New York's Harlem was the spiritual home of jazz. During the years 1910-1923 Leroy's jazz club had a strict no-whites policy. It is said that only one white man, Al Jolson, was made welcome during its thirteen years of operation.[2] *Conversely the original Cotton Club, also in Harlem, and which opened in 1923 had a whites-only policy even though most of the featured performers there were black! Musical geniuses such as Duke Ellington; Thomas 'Fats' Waller and Bessie Smith were regularly on the bill. Jolson made occasional guest appearances – usually on Sundays.*

On 5-6th June, 1920 *Sinbad* played at Spokane's Auditorium theatre in Washington State. In the audience for one of the performances was a teenage Harry Lillis (Bing) Crosby. The experience of seeing Jolson perform stayed with him all throughout his life. Years later Bing recounted the event in his 1953 autobiography, *Call Me Lucky*. "Jolson came through Spokane at least twice I think, in *Sinbad* and then *Bombo*. When I was 16 or 17 I would get a job in the Property Department of the theatre where they sent me on errands and the like. I always made sure I got the job when Jolson came. I picked up a lot from his stage persona – his deportment, and his singing. When he came on he was just 'electric', and he communicated this enthusiasm to the audience, so much so that they just wouldn't let him off". In his book Bing says that years later, when he got to know Al, they recalled those far off days and laughed. "He didn't remember the lop-eared lad called Crosby who watched his every move, but I remembered him vividly".[3] In 1972 Crosby also related the event to Michael Parkinson (Parkinson, BBC TV., 1972).

When you watch Bing Crosby singing in any of his old films, or even on the stage of the London Palladium, although very subtle, you can pick out the Jolson-inspired body language. There were also slight traces of Jolson in his singing (he never 'sang like Jolson' but the Jolson slurring, whistling and song-speech are evident – especially in his latter years). Bing was also working towards an innovative concept of voice production. He sought melodic and rhythmic liberation in order to sing more intimately, more conversationally. In this he was guided, as Jolson had been guided before him, by the Afro-American, also Jewish, oratorical concept of song. He also employed mannerisms, head-shaking, and would sometimes lapse into dialect à la Jolson. Jazz pundit and Crosby biographer, Gary Giddins, attributes this to 'vaudeville'. Clearly, Giddins had never studied Jolson.

Bing's most original contribution was the lowering of the voice, not so much in pitch as in intensity, to a conversational level.

Ethel Waters (1896-1977) was one of the first, black, recording artists. She began her career touring on the black vaudeville circuit working alongside the likes of Bessie Smith. Henry Pleasants tells us: *Along with Bessie Smith and Louis Armstrong, she was a fountainhead of all that is finest and most distinctive in American popular singing. As a singer she was a transitional figure, and a towering one, summing up all that had been accumulated stylistically from minstrel show, ragtime and coon song, and anticipating the artful, jazz-touched*

Afro-American inflections of the swing era. She was one of the first and, after Bessie Smith, probably the best of the many excellent singers who made race records and sang to black audiences in nightclubs and theatres across the country throughout the 1920s.

Ethel Waters and Eubie Blake: Courtesy of Henry Pleasants.

Unlike Smith, Water's singing was more than a little touched by white example. During the early 1920s she would frequent the jazz clubs of Harlem, the same clubs often visited by the likes of Al Jolson (perhaps with the exception of *Edmond's Cellar*, which Waters described as being 'The lowest rung of the entertainment world ladder'). During this period Ethel formed her association with Fletcher *'Smack'* Henderson, who provided her accompaniment. Ethel Waters had a, sometimes lovely, always expressive, but otherwise unexceptional voice. On her 1930 recording of 'Memories of You', she sounds almost like a cross between Jolson and Fanny Brice. And as with Jolson, who always dismembered the word melody, as in *mel-o-dee*; so with Waters when she sang memories – *mem-or-eees*.

It is a measure of Ethel Water's stature that the consensus among jazz critics is that she wasn't just a jazz singer, she was more than that. She was a great singer.[4]

Sources & Notes to Chapter Two:

1. Tenor: History of a Voice; John Potter (2010).

2. Per Chris Albertson's book: Bessie – Empress of the Blues (1894 – 1937). Bessie Smith was, arguably, the greatest female blues singer. Janis Joplin said of her: 'She showed me the air and taught me how to fill it'.

3. With acknowledgements to and paraphrased from Call Me Lucky. Bing Crosby and Pete Martin (1953).

4. With acknowledgements to and paraphrased from The Great American Popular Singers by Henry Pleasants, 1974 (Ref.2).

Authors note: As of 1989, Broadway was 'alive' with Jazz. Street musicians and jazz combos abounded. I was told these same musicians had named the city - the Big Apple.

CHAPTER THREE

A *showbiz* institution that was conceived from the opening of the Winter Garden Theatre (March, 1911) was the *Sunday Night Concerts*. Theatrical performances were illegal on Sundays. Producers would circumvent the law by putting on so-called 'sacred concerts', where performers would entertain in evening clothes, but without make-up. These concerts became popular with show folk (actors, agents and managers who would normally be working through the week). Here, according to Eddie Cantor, was Jolson at his best: "Oh, there would occasionally be others on the stage – a line of dancing girls – enough of a company to keep things going while Jolie took a sip of water, or to mop his brow off stage". Attired in a tuxedo, Al would entertain for around thirty minutes, then would strip off his collar and open his shirt, thereby anticipating the relaxation of social protocol and standards of decorum that would be characteristic of the jazz age. He became the entertainer's entertainer and as such, became established.

The next Jolson show was *Bombo,* another Sigmund Romberg musical and yet another 'extravaganza'. It was set in two time periods, the 1920s where Gus was the cook for a young explorer, and then in 1492 in which Gus became Bombo, the servant of Christopher Columbus. The show was originally scheduled to open at the Winter Garden but the Shubert's wanted that theatre as a flagship for their foray into vaudeville. They moved the opening of *Bombo* to the new Imperial Theatre on 59th street. By way of a sweetener they offered to rename the house as Jolson's 59th Street Theatre.

Front elevation of Jolson's 59th Street Theatre: Shubert Archive; ibdb.com/theatre/new-century-theatre-1220

At 35 Al Jolson would become the youngest man in history to have a theatre named after him. The show opened on Thursday night, 6th October 1921. So successful was that opening night that Al took thirty-seven curtain calls. (Ref.1)

Located at 932 Seventh Avenue in Midtown Manhattan the Jolson Theatre, built in 1921, had a seating capacity of 1700 (slightly more than the Winter Garden). Over the years it underwent several name changes, being originally designed for the Shubert Organisation it has subsequently been - Central Park Theatre; Shakespeare Theatre; Venice Theatre; Jolson's 59th Street Theatre (again); Molly Picon Theatre; Jolson's. . .(again) and finally the New Century Theatre (1944 – 54). Notable productions are: *Bombo* (1921); *The Student Prince*, 1924; *The Cradle Will Rock*, 1937; *Kiss Me Kate* (1948 and longest running) and *Out Of This World* by Cole Porter (1950). The place closed in 1954 and was demolished in 1962. *Bombo* ran at the 59th Street Theatre for six months.

Chapter Three

It was in *Bombo* that Jolson first sang the song that he later described as his second favourite - *April Showers*. Written by Buddy De Sylva and Louis Silvers it was to prove another *Bombo* showstopper. When singing the number he would point to the gallery and proclaim, "Look, look, they're not clouds, no, no – they're crowds of – daffodils", the packed auditorium would be in a near frenzy. *Bombo* turned out to be the most spectacular show in which he had yet appeared.*

In the summer of 1923 a 20-years old Ralph Reader had just arrived in New York from England to try his luck on the American Stage. One afternoon he decided to catch a performance of *Bombo*. Upon turning up at the box office, and to his chagrin, he read a sign on the door which stated that there would be no matinee that day as Mr Jolson was taking the entire company to the races! He remembers thinking to himself, what sort of arrogant performer would cancel a performance just to take the cast to see horse racing? As it turned out he managed to secure a ticket for the evening performance. Having sat through the show, which he classed as the most moving night of his whole life, he couldn't go home so he just walked around Central Park until his head cleared. In a personal letter received from Mr Reader in 1979, he told me that he'd never been so emotional about anybody or anything, in his entire life.

Ralph Reader, CBE, while only 21 had choreographed his first Broadway show (*Artists and Models*), prompting the *New York Times* to print: 'Watch Ralph Reader'. Upon returning to England he produced several West End productions. He is chiefly remembered for the Boy Scout Gang Shows.

In the meantime Jolson continued to make recordings and was almost talked into starring in a silent movie. After a run of more than 200 consecutive performances, *Bombo* closed.

---

* Michael Freedland.

Promotional poster for the Charlie Chaplin film The Vagabond (1916).
CC0 1.0 Universal

CHAPTER FOUR

It was also during this era that a diminutive comic actor from England had firmly established himself in the hearts of the American public. [Sir] Charles Spencer Chaplin, born in London in 1889, came to the USA with the Fred Karno's outfit. Chaplin's childhood had closely paralleled Jolson's, both had been reared in poverty, hardship, and institutions, both had their introduction to the entertainment world *via* music hall. The *Tramp* persona that Chaplin invented was also, in some ways, similar to Jolson's *Gus*. Slapstick combined with pathos and the struggles with adversity, but always coming off best. But more importantly, both artists' biographers believed that when in character they actually became that character. By 1918 Charlie was a global phenomenon, possibly Hollywood's first international star. Also in 1918 Chaplin was visited by [Sir] Harry Lauder and the two appeared in a short subject together. Sir Harry was one of the two performers that Jolson said he admired, the other was W. C. Fields. The following year Charlie co-founded the distribution company, United Artists, along with Mary Pickford, Douglas Fairbanks and D. W. Griffith. This gave them complete artistic control over their films. Chaplin's first feature-length opus was *The Kid*, made in 1921 with Jackie Coogan as the Kid. Interestingly, some years later, United Artists made a picture starring Jolson in which he appeared as head honcho over a band of New York tramps who hung out in the city's Central Park. The film became 'the big experiment', the dialogue was written entirely in rhyming couplets with music and lyrics by Rodgers and Hart. Typically, Jolson, in his support for black talent, chose black actor Edgar Connor as his sidekick. The film, *Hallelujah I'm a Bum,* bombed. This was despite Mordaunt Hall of the *New York Times* saying it was 'Jolson's best film'. Regina Crewe of the *American* called it a 'Triumph'. Al Jolson's only art film was a box office flop.

Charlie Chaplin, left, with Al Jolson in 1928: International Al Jolson Society.

The early 1920s ushered in what became known as *The Jazz Age*. This coincided with the change from acoustic to electronic recording techniques. It was at this time that Al switched from Columbia to the Brunswick label. It was also around this time that the theme of his recordings saw a shift from *ragtime* to *hot jazz*. It was now the era dominated by Vincent Youmans and George Gershwin. Youmans collaborated with virtually all the great Broadway lyricists. Perhaps his best known work of the 1920s was *No, No, Nanette* with Irving Caesar. *(The show is best remembered for the song, Tea for Two. It became the preferred tune of anyone learning to dance the Cha-cha-cha)* One hot jazz number, and a particular favourite, that Jolson recorded during the twenties is, *Tonight's My Night with Baby.* With risqué words by Irving

Caesar, it tells of a man who is 'on a promise'. Definitely pre-Code, *viz*. *"We've seen every movie, we've seen every play, we gotta have amusement but we want it in a different way"*. Also, *"The onions that I love so much, for weeks I haven't dared to touch – tonight's my night with Baby"*. Another 'bobby-dazzler' and recorded on March 14, 1924 is *Home in Pasadena*.

Among the many Jolson-inspired jazz recordings to emerge during the decade were: *My Mammy's Blues* by Reb Spikes and his Majors and Minors; *My Sweetie Turned Sour on Me* (Dubin's Dandies); *Swanee Shuffle* – Duke Ellington and his orchestra, also *Saint Louis Blues* by Cab Calloway (Calloway's 1931 recording – *Minnie the Moocher* was the first single by an African-American artist to sell one million copies).

The 1920s also saw the emergence of Paul *'Pops'* Whiteman and his orchestra. Whiteman, previously a violist, and later referred to as the 'King of Jazz', formed his band in 1921 and they popularised a musical style that helped to introduce jazz to mainstream audiences during the decade under review. The Whiteman orchestra was a training ground and platform for aspiring vocalists and jazz soloists; Bing Crosby[*], Bix Beiderbecke (arguably the first, great, white jazz musician), Mildred Bailey and Joe Venuti, to name but four. Like Jolson, Paul Whiteman's place in the history of jazz is somewhat controversial[**]. His critics suggest that his ornately orchestrated music was jazz in name only. One critic accused him of 'trying to make a Lady out of jazz', while British jazz musician, Benny Green, dismisses him as 'vaudeville'. Paul Whiteman is perhaps best remembered today for his orchestration of the Gershwin jazz classic – *Rhapsody in Blue*.

---

[*] Garry Giddins maintains that some of Crosby's best recordings were made with Pops Whiteman
[**] It is fashionable nowadays to sneer at any association of Al Jolson with jazz. That he should have made history with a picture called *The Jazz Singer* is thought of as an appalling joke, even more appalling than Paul Whiteman's figurative coronation as '*the King of Jazz*'. This is to judge a man who was already thirty-four, possibly older, in 1920 by the jazz standards of those who, when Jolson was thirty-four, had not been born. It would seem also to assume that jazz began with Sidney Bechet, King Oliver and Louis Armstrong. It is to think in terms of jazz, however defined, rather than in terms of an Afro-American idiom in whose evolution the jazz of Bechet, Oliver and Armstrong was only an episode. (Ref.2).

In his book, *The Great American Popular Singers*, Henry Pleasants tells us that a combination of circumstances conspired in the 1920s to revolutionise both popular song and popular singing:

> *Popular music had been absorbing and reflecting black influences for nearly a century. There was always an interchange, a process of imitation and counter imitation, or parody. Blacks originally imitated – or parodied – the manners and speech of their white masters. The imperfect result was thought by whites to be amusing – and so charming – that they parodied the imitation for their own amusement. The phenomenon of imitation breeding imitation is documented in the century long history of the minstrel show. First, whites blacked their faces to imitate blacks imitating whites. Then blacks followed suit in their own minstrel shows, blacking their already black faces to imitate whites imitating blacks. This naïve, unselfconscious give-and-take bore fruit in the work of many popular singers of the 1920s and before. A kind of song and a kind of singing, most vividly and most memorably represented by Sophie Tucker and Al Jolson, were enormously popular. One winces today when recalling that the songs were called 'coon songs' and the style of singing 'coon shouting'. By the early 1920s the more common designation was 'blues', which did not mean, then, the classic twelve-bar form associated with the term today. It was simply a jazzy or bluesy popular song evolving from the slow transition from ragtime to jazz. What is important to remember is that these songs were written by both black and white songwriters and sung by both black - and white singers* (Ref 2).

Paul Whiteman and Al Jolson came together again in 1933 (their first radio collaboration had been in 1928), when the Kraft Music Hall [originally the Kraft Program] was launched on the NBC network. Commercial radio was big in the USA at the time and paid well. The two-hour programme went out weekly and starred Paul Whiteman and his orchestra with Jolson as guest artist. Kraft-Phoenix were so impressed with the reviews that they offered Al the starring role at $5,000 per broadcast. He was signed to do 26 one-hour shows from August, 3rd that year. From 1936 Bing Crosby took over the reins of the broadcast, remaining *in situ* for ten years. Then, from 1947, Jolson again resumed control.

The year 1924 was key in the development of the American musical theatre. In fact the modern musical actually 'took off' as composers, backed by ASCAP,[1] had gained the right to control scores.

King of Jazz; Paul 'Pops' Whiteman and his orchestra dominated the recording industry during the 1920s

The earlier practice of interpolating numbers was abandoned. Extravaganzas, like the Jolson musicals, began to look old-fashioned in the new world of Gershwin and Youmans. It was in the same year that Jolson finally succumbed to the pestering of silent film-maker, D. W. Griffith (*Birth of a Nation*). Al could never see what attributes he could bring to silent film. The gambler in him obviously came to the fore and he eventually relented but insisted there be no contract. The film was to be called Mammy's Boy or Black Magic. However, Jolson was so appalled after seeing the first rushes of himself in a non-singing role that he immediately absconded to Europe on board the liner *RMS Majestic*.[2]

The next Jolson show was *Big Boy*, a musical comedy based on the play, *In Old Kentucky*. It went into rehearsals in October, 1924 with the young Englishman, Ralph Reader, in the chorus. *Big Boy* toured for six weeks before opening in New York. Because *The Student Prince* was enjoying a successful run at Jolson's 59th Street Theatre, *Big Boy* opened at the Winter Garden on the night of January 7th 1925. The show's plot had ruthless gamblers conspiring to have Gus fired from Bedford Stables so that their own jockey could ride Big Boy and throw the Kentucky Derby. Gus eventually susses the scam, thwarts their actions, and goes on to ride *Big Boy* to victory. *(Years later one of the pit musicians confirmed the story about Big Boy dumping while on stage, prompting Jolson to quip, "It's a good thing he's not an elephant!")*. Al Jolson in *Big Boy* drew what is still the greatest critical acclaim for a musical comedy. The humourist, Robert Benchley, one-time member of the famous Algonquin Round Table, noted the following in *Life* magazine: "To sit and feel the lift of Jolson's personality is to know what the coiners of the word 'personality' meant. The word isn't quite strong enough for the thing that Jolson has. Unimportant as the comparison may be to Mr Jolson, we should say that John the Baptist was the last man to possess such a power. .". Notwithstanding, the audience saw a more sophisticated, urbane Jolson than before. The show grossed $5,000 per performance (compared to the *Ziegfeld Follies* $3,000 – a show loaded with talent, beautiful girls and of course, Eddie Cantor). Despite all the accolades, there were times when the Jolson 'hypochondria' would surface again – usually in the guise of laryngitis. Pre-booked performances of

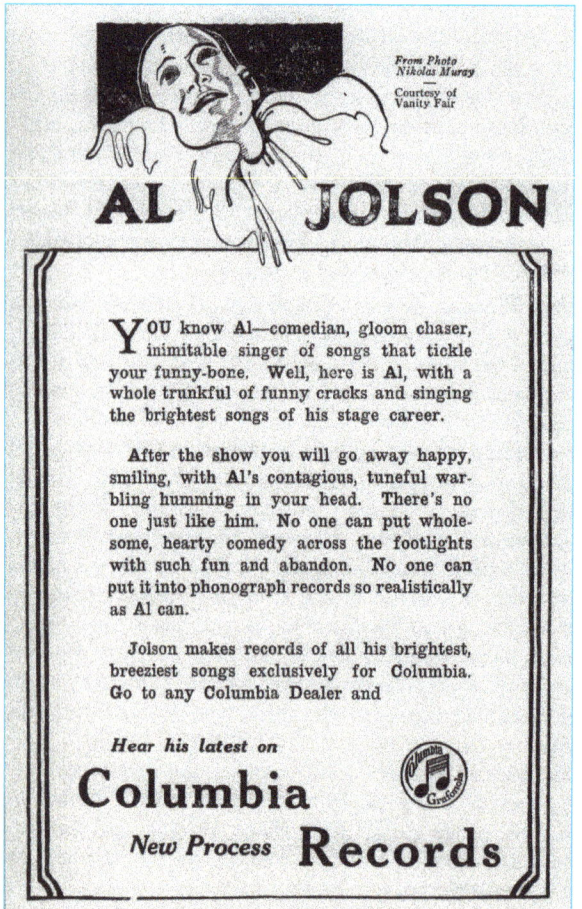

Big Boy would have to be cancelled resulting in the Shuberts accusing Al of feigning illness. Jolson had surrounded himself with a coterie of N.Y. doctors who, erring on the side of caution, would insist that he took himself off to Miami or Palm Springs, 'for a good rest'. Herb Goldman suggests that if Al's medical team had included a psychiatrist, then his real problem may have been addressed.

From March 20, 1926 Jolson started a four week gig as star guest in the Winter Garden revue – *Artists and Models*. The show being the Shubert's answer to the *Ziegfeld Follies*. There were completely nude girls on stage but the Jolson celebrity was sufficient to take the audience's attention off of the mountains of flesh on display. Later he took the show to Chicago. There, in a week, it grossed $60,400, more than any other show in the history of the stage. Herbert Goldman notes that April 24, 1926 marks Jolson's last performance at the New York Winter Garden (ref 1).

Notes to Chapter Four:

1 ASCAP: The American Society of Composers, Authors and Publishers, founded in 1914, is a non-profit organisation that protects its member's copyrights.

2 Before the days of long-haul air travel the only way to cross the Atlantic Ocean was by ship. Jolson made several trans-Atlantic crossings, usually with one of his wives, to France. And in the first-class splendour of the following liners, *RMS Berengaria; RMS Mauretania; RMS Majestic; SS Leviathan; RMS Olympic* (sister ship to the Titanic and, at the time, the largest liner in the world). In 1930 a Caribbean cruise, *via* Bermuda, was undertaken on the *RMSP Araguaya*. [Asa Yoelson first came to the USA, *via* Liverpool, in 1894 aboard the *RMS Umbria,* the last liner to be fitted with auxiliary sails].

Poster for the movie The Jazz Singer (1927), featuring stars Eugenie Besserer and Al Jolson. Warner Bros. (original rights holder)

CHAPTER FIVE

The year 1927 was an eventful one in the history of the USA. The Stock Market was booming; television was invented; it was the peak of Capone's reign of terror and the return to greatness of baseball player Babe Ruth. Then there was the solo flight of Charles Lindbergh. Oh, and also the birth of talking pictures. [1]

The starring role in *The Jazz Singer* was first offered to Georgie Jessel who was playing the part in a stage version. Jessel missed out because he, allegedly, demanded too high a fee. The reality was probably that he was frightened to take the risk, worrying about the effect it would have on his career if the 'experiment' flopped. The same would also apply to Eddie Cantor, who was also offered the part. At the time when Warners got together with Western Electric to found the Vitaphone Corporation (April, 1926), Jolson was still touring with *Big Boy*. While in Denver, he was approached by a Warner's executive and offered *The Jazz Singer* lead. Herb Goldman tells us that the myth was perpetuated that Jolie took all or part of his salary in Warner's stock (he was paid $75,000). Warner's did not offer him any stock, neither did he put up any of his own money – as has often been claimed.

The Vitaphone talking pictures process was virtually out of date when it was being invented! The sound-on-film process of Lee DeForest was being developed contemporaneously. *(Sound on film is the technique that is used today)*. The problem with it during the mid-twenties was that the sound quality was not as good as Vitaphone's sound-on-disc system. Vitaphone involved the use of large records that were synchronised to the camera with a flexible cable. The drawback was that, for instance if, say, a large vehicle drove past the studio, the vibration could cause the stylus to jump a groove putting the recording 'out of sync'. Extraneous noise was also a problem, so the recording equipment had to be housed in a sound-proof booth. From today's standpoint it all looks very primitive. Filming of The Jazz Singer began on July 11th after *Big Boy* closed in 'Frisco.

Jolson's co-star, May McAvoy, later stated, "It was his first picture, and he was like a little boy. He was frightened to death. He was really frightened".

Prior to the start of filming Jolson had arrived by train in Hollywood. He was met at the station by Jack, Harry and Sam Warner, also Daryl Zanuck. He hadn't been there long before other stars came to greet him. Charlie Chaplin and Douglas Fairbanks were happy to pose for photos with him. They were obviously unaware what effect this one man would have on their industry. If Jolson himself had any thoughts on the matter, it is doubtful he realised that he might be creating a monster. Chaplin announced in the press that he would never make a sound picture, causing Jolson to make the following comment during an interview. "The talkies are not going to spoil the art of pantomime. If Chaplin wants to keep what he calls 'the great beauty of silence', let him go lock himself in a room – or become a nun's brother, or something. Ha, we were at a party together the other night and from 8.30 to around 5am Charlie never shut up. I think Chaplin is great, but why not become greater by doing something the public wants him to do?" *It is now general knowledge that Chaplin did eventually go on to make 'talkies'.*

The Jazz Singer premiered at the Warner's Theatre in New York City and played to huge crowds, even at the premium price of $10 per ticket. It consigned the silent movie to the bonfire and destroyed careers virtually overnight. Faces which had previously sent millions of women into swoons belonged to voices which would now transport them into hysterics. It is obviously difficult, from our present standpoint, to appreciate just how much of a culture shock the arrival of sound would be. May McAvoy later recalled that she would stand in cinemas where it was showing and watch the audiences. "When Jolson spoke", she said, "people reacted with such rapture, you'd have thought they were listening to the voice of God".

It is not the intention to delve into the history of radio nor the microphone, suffice to say that the emergence of both seriously changed vocal techniques and the articulation of song. By late 1922, in the United States, there were some 3,000,000 sets being serviced by more than 200 transmitters; then by 1925, radio was an $800,000,000-a-year industry. This environment paved the way for a style of vocalising called *crooning*. Early exponents were Russ Columbo, Gene Austin, Whispering Jack Smith and Rudy Vallee. (Al Jolson was once asked during a radio interview what he thought of Rudy Vallee. "Rudy Vallee", he quipped. "Where's that?"). One of these early crooners was our friend Bing Crosby. With his mastery of the art he would soon be head and shoulders above the rest. He has been called the first *cool* white man in America. No other singer has been so deceptive, so free of artistic pretentions, and so inadequately assessed. Many people, who only know him from such as the perennial *White Christmas* or *Where the Blue of the Night*, may

Bing Crosby with Jolson at the races, 1938: Barrie Anderton/Jupiter Books.

be surprised to learn that he was a very capable jazz singer, being comfortable with excursions into scat singing *(a white man scatting!)*. Benny Green, when on BBC radio, always lamented Bing's recording choices (inferior material). It transpired that this was down to Decca Records chief, Jack Kapp. Bing was under contract to Decca, and Kapp knew what was commercial.

Si Si Si Senor: How Jolson may have looked in A Night in Spain?
International Al Jolson Society, JJ.132

In January 1928 Al made his radio debut on the *Dodge Victory Hour* (the special one hour broadcast also included Paul Whiteman). In March 1928 he made his first (non-pc) recording of the classic, *Old Man River* from

Show Boat that had opened the previous year. Jolson would later refer to Jerome Kern, the song's composer, as the dean of American music. Later in March he appeared in the review, *A Night in Spain* at Chicago's Four Cohans Theatre. For the four-week stint he received $50,000, it remained a record salary paid to anyone in the legitimate theatre for many years. Following his appearance in *A Night in Spain*, Jolson went back to Hollywood, this time to star in another Warner's picture for a fee of $500,000 – more than six times what he had been paid for The Jazz Singer.

Filming began on *The Singing Fool* (another part-talkie) during the summer of 1928. The film contained several of his old numbers and a new song entitled *There's a Rainbow 'Round My Shoulder*. There was, however, still one song to be written that Al would 'croon' to his Sonny Boy. Jolson contacted the song-writing team of DeSylva, Brown and Henderson – the top pop writers of the day - who were working in Atlantic City, and outlined his requirement. Jolson provided them with the first line, *viz.* "Climb upon my knee Sonny Boy, tho' you're only three Sonny Boy". The song-writing trio contributed the rest, allegedly, as a joke. It must have been the most corny, banal lyric that they ever wrote (although the melody is quite good). Jolson loved it. Jazz critic, Benny Green said, "Can you imagine it taking three men to write this? Perhaps they took turns in holding each other up?" Actually, Jolson's name also appeared among the writer's credits and so, in effect, it took the combined efforts of four men! Al sang the number three times in the film, it became an instant hit[*] selling more than one million copies. *Sonny Boy* became the most commercially successful song of Al Jolson's long career. It actually ranks, according to Benny Green, as perhaps one of a half-dozen most successful and influential vocal recordings of all-time. Years later when entertaining US service personnel during World War Two, and after

---

[*] That Al Jolson could make a hit out of a corny ditty such as Sonny Boy is testament to his artistry. He could have wooed audiences reciting a laundry list. Frank Sinatra, on the other hand, needed to have music and lyrics out of the top-drawer, otherwise his performance suffered. That was the difference between these two great artists.

receiving a request to sing *Sonny Boy*, Al stated, "I don't like to sing Sonny Boy too much, its sentimental all right but it's as corny as a deuce, the only thing it ever did for me, with the royalties, I bought a home in Florida, outside of that nothing".

As for the film itself, it remained the most successful ever made, until *Gone with the Wind* eclipsed it ten years later.

During the 1970s I remember getting into arguments with old-timers who insisted The Singing Fool *was actually the first talkie, and they had seen it – at Barrow's Coliseum Theatre! I found myself explaining to them that when* The Jazz Singer *came out a lot of theatres were not 'wired for sound', but twelve months later, when* The Singing Fool *was released, they obviously were.*

First Day Cover marking 50 years of Talking Pictures: S. Henderson.

Notes to Chapter Five:

1 Paraphrased from *One Summer. . .* Bill Bryson (2013).

CHAPTER SIX

Between the years 1904 to 1939 Al Jolson had lived at several addresses in the *Big Apple*, as well as having homes in Florida and California. His Cinderella-like, rags to riches, story saw him going from a room in the hotel *Trafalgar*, at 115-117 East Fourteenth Street – which he described as being little more than a broom cupboard – to the luxury and opulence of the *Ritz Tower* on Park Avenue, and also the *Sherry-Netherland Apartment Hotel* on Fifth Avenue. When it was built in 1927 the Sherry-Netherland was the tallest apartment-hotel in the City. In between touring in *Big Boy*, Al may have possibly witnessed the spectacular fire that broke out and engulfed the upper floors on April 12, 1927. An estimated one hundred thousand people gathered to see the spectacle which would prove embarrassing for the NY Fire Department, as their hoses couldn't reach the upper floors of the building.

Early in 1928, Al had become aware of a young dancer at Texas Guinan's El Fey Club (a speakeasy on West 47th Street) in the City. The petite 18-years old Ruby Keeler caught his fancy but he was unaware, at the time, that she was, in fact, a gangster's moll! Ruby was the girlfriend of one Johnny 'Irish' Costello, and he was heavily involved with the supply of illicit whiskey in the Manhattan district during Prohibition. Anyway, the upshot was that Jolson's persistence with Ruby won him the day and despite received threats, they wed and immediately embarked for France on the *RMS Olympic*. The superstar was not without influence, he never received any grief from the

Johnny Irish quarter. *[He did, however, settle a six-figure sum on Miss Keeler, apparently as a pre-wedding present. This, allegedly, had been agreed with the Mob]*. The Jolsons returned home from Europe on the SS. Leviathan. When the ship docked in New York, the quayside was awash with the press, who were anxious to pick-up any gossip and to take pictures of the celebrity couple.

The Jolsons on their return from Europe in 1928: National Film Archive.

In the summer of '29 Ruby had agreed to star in *Show Girl*, a Ziegfeld musical comedy based on the career of Broadway showgirl, Dixie Dugan. When the show went into rehearsals Al was three thousand miles away making his third film for Warners. The film, tentatively titled *Little Pal* but later changed to *Say it With Songs,* had Jolson *crooning* to his 'little pal', played by the same child actor who had been Sonny Boy in The Singing Fool (more than one film critic noticed the sameness of the offering, also Jolson's 'wooden' acting). The film would be the first professional flop of Al Jolson's long career. *Speaking on the BBC in 1976, Douglas Fairbanks Jnr. said, "what knocked them out on the back row in the theatre was one thing, but the screen, which can magnify an actor twenty or thirty times, requires someone that can 'underplay', restraint rather than exaggeration (as with Jolson's larger-than-life grimaces)".* According to Michael Freedland Jolson was made to measure for the big Hollywood musical - but he didn't get one. Producers were, it would seem, frightened of him. Studio bosses thinking, perhaps, that he would 'take over' as he did in his live shows! One thing is certain – given the right director (one who could handle him), Jolson the actor may have come to the fore. Glimpses of an improved acting ability became evident in later films such as in the 1939 *Fox Pictures, Rose of Washington Square and Swanee River.* Meanwhile, his next picture for Warners was almost ready for shooting.

In May 1929, the Jolsons attended the first Academy Awards (*Oscars*) ceremony at the Roosevelt Hotel in Los Angeles. The Academy of Motion Picture Arts and Sciences gave Warner Bros. a special award for producing *The Jazz Singer* – which Al accepted on behalf of the Studio.

Show Girl opened in Boston in June of 1929 for a pre-Broadway run. Ruby, by all accounts, was excellent in the part of Dixie and received an ovation for the number *Do what You Do*. The best song in the show was *Liza,* written by George and Ira Gershwin. *Liza* featured in the scene where there is an expanse of wide stairs right across the stage, Ruby made her entrance at the top of the stairway and into the spotlight as the orchestra struck up for the big number. Unbeknown to her Jolson was in the audience with Flo Ziegfeld. Right out of the blue he stood up from his seat and launched into the song, to the delight of the audience. The following day's reviews concentrated on Jolson's impromptu performance giving little or no credit to Ruby – whose show it was! The incident has since gone down in show business lore.

"Liza, Liza skies are grey. . ." Al working for nothing! Courtesy of Otis R. Lowe.

Mammy, the next Jolson picture, finished shooting just before the stock market crash of 1929. The film was novel in several ways. It featured a new score by Irving Berlin (including the standard, *Let Me Sing and I'm Happy*) and the number, *Looking at You* which Jolson interpreted in a conventional, European style, sounding almost like a *Jewish* John McCormack. The final reel was shot in Technicolor. *Mammy* was Warner Brothers' title for the stage show, *Mister Bones*. The trite plot had Al as an *end man* in a minstrel line-up accused of attempted murder. He runs away and hides at his mother's house in a tearful scene reminiscent of *The Jazz Singer*. In the film, Jolson shows himself as a masterful comedian, but his acting is embarrassing. The films' reviews were only lukewarm and it became his second flop.

The Wall Street Crash was the most devastating stock market crash in the history of the United States – following directly the crash of the London Stock Exchange. The event brought the Roaring Twenties, that decade of wealth and excess, to an abrupt halt. The crash and the Great Depression that followed formed the largest financial crisis of the 20th century. It was estimated that Al Jolson lost around one and a half million dollars*, almost half his total worth, but he took his losses philosophically. A gambler by nature, he viewed the making of money as a game.

During the spring of 1930, Jolson started filming *Big Boy* for Warners in between popping into the recording studio to cut records. By far his greatest effort in the medium that year was Irving Berlin's, *Let Me Sing and I'm Happy*, also the 'jazzy', *When the Little Red Roses get the Blues for You*. *Big Boy* was a film version of his successful 1925 stage show. It showcased Al (as Gus, the underdog who baited his adversaries at every opportunity), as an exciting singer also a sharp comedian. The film was in production just short of two months, opening on September 11, 1930 and is the only record of Al playing the character, Gus. It was also his last picture under his current contract with the Warners. It would be five years before he was back working at the Burbank Studio.

---

* Approximately $20 million in 2020.

Photo of Ethel 'Ruby' Keeler from the film Footlight Parade.

CHAPTER SEVEN

Al Jolson's survival into the *swing era* had been an uphill and eventually, a losing battle. The beginning of the era coincided with his decision to cease making commercial recordings (December 1932). In February 1933 he made his last radio broadcast for Chevrolet after which he, allegedly, threw his microphone to the floor saying, *"It's a sad day when Jolie needs a mike to sing into!"* Meanwhile Ruby was still working on the film *Gold Diggers* followed by *Forty-Second Street.* Ruby Keeler-Jolson had firmly established herself as the naïve ingénue who tap-danced her way into everyone's hearts and almost instant stardom. *The New York Herald Tribune* noted: "Ruby Keeler is rather more valuable as a cinema player than her celebrated husband, Al Jolson". *I am reminded at this point to draw a parallel with Bing Crosby who, in 1930, married his first wife, Dixie Lee. Dixie at the time was more of a headliner than Bing, to the extent that one reporter noted in the local press that film star Dixie Lee had married crooner, Bing Croveny!* [1]

Al had become a victim of technology. Talking Pictures, the monster he had helped to create, was now consuming him. They had assassinated vaudeville and diminished the importance of the legitimate theatre.[2] His abilities and talent were not suited to the movies - he felt uncomfortable in front of the camera and his acting fell short of what was required (had the studios put him in more appropriate vehicles, *i.e.* comedies, the Jolson film career might have been different. But Jolson in films would still not have been Jolson in the theatre). Herbert Goldman also tells us that, "The sad fact was that *Jolie* did not register very well in any mechanical medium". However, despite his *virile* style of singing being out of date, he retained his 'talent to amuse'. Throughout most of the thirties, he still had a top-rated radio show. The irony is that on these shows he introduced several songs for the very first time [standards] that would later be put on disc by others. All in all the 1930s was a fabulous era for Hollywood, and also for song writing. If the reader will indulge me here, I would like to list a handful of personal favourites from the decade: *About a Quarter to Nine; Begin the Beguine; Cheek to Cheek; Dancing in the Dark; Once in A While; Night and Day; September in the Rain* and *You Are Too Beautiful.*

Harry Warren [1893-1981] was, arguably, the most prolific composer during the era of the 1930's film musical. He was the first major songwriter to write primarily for film. Hubert Gregg tells us that Warren wrote many first-class tunes for many second rate films! Born Salvatore Guaragna in Brooklyn, New York, his name had been changed to Warren before he could pronounce the first! Warren collaborated with many lyricists, including Al Dubin; Ira Gershwin; Mack Gordon and Johnny Mercer. A particular favourite of mine is Warren and Dubin's, *Don't Say Good-Night* (vocalised by Dick Powell), the big production number, choreographed by Busby Berkeley and used to good effect in the 1934 film – *Wonder Bar*.[3]

For Al Jolson the thirties would be a decade of frustration, culminating in his divorce from Ruby Keeler. With the swing era, following the rise of radio and phonograph records, power had shifted to the bandleaders (and to some extent, the band singers). The end of the decade would see the emergence of a singer who would eventually make a serious bid for Crosby's crown.[4]

Al Jolson appeared in his last outing for the Shubert Brothers, it would seem, because of pressure from Lee Shubert. The brothers claimed he had broken the terms of his contract by walking out of *Big Boy* in 1927. They would, however, consider dropping the suit if he agreed to star in a show they were planning in association with theatrical producer, Morris Gest. Jolson agreed and also bought a half interest in the show - which was called *The Wonder Bar* being based on *Der Wunderbar* (pronounced Vunderbar), which had opened in Vienna. It was described as 'A Continental novelty of European nightlife'. The Shuberts originally had Broadway performer, Harry Richman in mind, but when they couldn't agree terms, Lee suggested Jolson. (Richman had previously introduced *Puttin' on the Ritz* in the 1930 film of the same name). Upon becoming involved, Jolson brought in Irving Caesar who, at the time, was living in Al's suite in the *Ritz Tower*. Caesar re-wrote the *libretto,* structuring it to accommodate Jolson as *Monsieur* Al, he also adapted several numbers from the original score. The title song, *Vunderbar* became *Good Evening, Friends,* he also included *A Chazend'l Ohf Chabbes* (The Cantor) a Yiddish folk song. Caesar also had Jolson sing his *Oh Donna Clara* – in three languages!

Al Jolson and Morris Gest snapped while discussing the show's libretto: courtesy of Marc I. Leavey, M.D.

The Wonder Bar previewed in Washington DC on March 5, 1931. It then had its Broadway opening on March 17th at the Nora Bayes Theatre in New York. It is not remembered as Jolson's greatest show – and there was no Gus!

The Bayes Theatre was located at 216 West 44th Street, it had previously been Weber and Fields' Music Hall.

Al at the bar having a pre-show cocktail: Marc I. Leavey, M.D.

A theatre on the roof of the building became the Bayes Theatre in 1918. (During Prohibition the basement was occupied by a speakeasy). Notable productions following *The Wonder Bar*, are: Face the Music (1933); Four Saints in Three Acts (1934); Winged Victory (1943) and On the Town (1945). From 1942 it became the location for the original *Stage Door Canteen* then, in 1945, the building was demolished. (*Wiki*)

On opening nights Al Jolson was said to be like a maniac! Samson Raphaelson always maintained that he came on stage 'like a duck hitting water'. The opening number, *Good Evening (Friends)*, saw *emcee*, Monsieur Al belting out a multi-lingual 'welcome' to the seated clientele. In doing so anticipating the *emcee* from *Cabaret (singing Willkommen)*, by about thirty-five years.

The Wonder Bar, set in 1930s Paris, and *Cabaret's Kit Kat Klub* (1930s Berlin). Were both seedy nightspots, described as places of decadent celebration?

"Good evening all you socialites, and all you gay suburbanites, how be ya? Happy to see ya". Oscar Cesare cartoon depicting Al Jolson, as emcee, in The Wonder Bar. Published in The New York Times, March 29, 1931. Courtesy of Marc I. Leavey, M.D.

The reviews for *The Wonder Bar* were not the usual Jolson raves. Several critics thought him uncomfortable in his role as proprietor-cum-emcee. Writing in the *Brooklyn Eagle*, critic Arthur Pollard said his role gave him no springboard from which to leap to success. Al was reportedly extremely nervous during the show's Broadway run, so much so that buckets had to be placed in the wings so that he could retch after finishing his scenes *(Ref.1)*. When the matinee receipts began to drop, Al's throat, predictably, began to hurt, so on May 30th, the show closed. [5] For a while, he consoled himself at the race track.

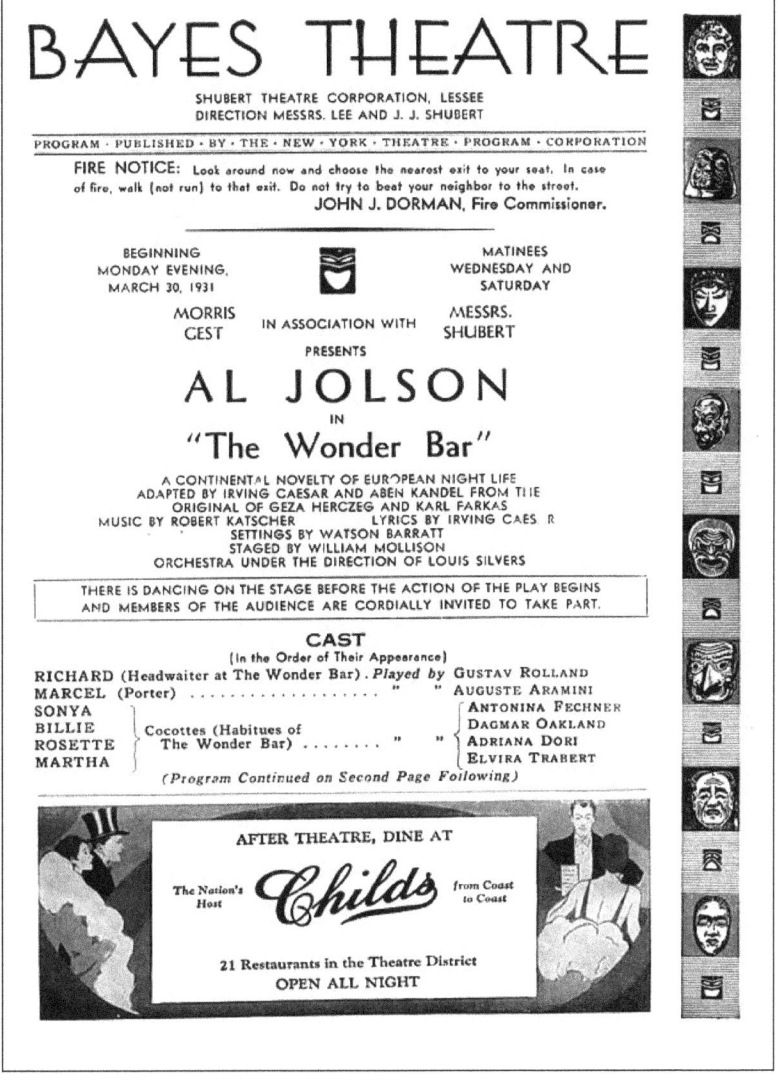

Playbill for The Wonder Bar: Courtesy of Marc I. Leavey, M.D.

It was during the New York run of *The Wonder Bar*, according to Michael Freedland, that Al met with the opera singer, Fyodor Chaliapin (1873 – 1938), both had been Russian émigrés. Chaliapin, a giant of a man, was probably the greatest *basso-profundo* who ever lived. Freedland tells us that Chaliapin was so impressed with Al's rendition of *Oh Donna Clara*, he suggested he and 'Arll' spend some quality time together. Quality time that would include girls and vodka, as Irving Caesar later recalled.

For the next three months, the *Mighty Jolson* was professionally inactive, although he did spend some of the summer fishing off Catalina Island, not far from his beloved *Avalon*.[6] Towards the end of August he and Ruby headed back to New York where Louis Epstein* (his then manager), had made all the necessary arrangements for Al to take *The Wonder Bar* on tour. Epstein, by all accounts, had excelled himself in negotiating the terms of Al's contract. A six-thousand dollar weekly guarantee with a starting point of 50 percent of the show's profits plus extras. This figure was the absolute top rate paid to anyone, including – according to Goldman – Sarah Bernhardt, and only granted because producers knew no one else would ever do the necessary business. Martin Fried, a former rehearsal pianist, replaced Louis Silvers as Al's conductor.

The show opened in Newark, NJ on September 18th, 1931, and then, during the next six months, it played in almost forty cities across the North American continent. By 1932 Jolson had slipped but was still a bankable asset. In Des Moines, Iowa, on February 23rd, *The Wonder Bar* grossed what Epstein claimed was an all-time high for a Broadway musical - $16,000 in Depression money! During the show's tour of '*the sticks*', Jolson recalled, "I spent nearly all my spare time gargling".

The Wonder Bar tour ended at the Curran Theatre in San Francisco on April 9th, 1932. It was time for Al to report to United Artists and Lewis Milestone.

---

* Louis Epstein – who had taught Al how to whistle – would later become Mae West's manager. He also discovered the comedy duo Abbott & Costello. Ref.1

We conclude our tour of the highlights of Al's Broadway years by reprising what Benny Green said when marking the 70th birthday of Frank Sinatra in December, 1985. "Sinatra never lost the conviction that New York was what really mattered, despite being raised on the eastern seaboard but finding fame and fortune in California. You could become a Hollywood big shot or a Beverly Hills lion, but if they didn't rate you on Broadway, where were you?"

Notes to Chapter Seven:

1 *Bing Crosby: the illustrated biography,* Michael Freedland, 1998.

2 One of the first casualties of sound films was *Show Boat* (1927). When it went on tour in 1929, everyone was going to the pictures [talkies]. Composer, Jerome Kern never had another hit on Broadway after *Show Boat,* and like so many others, he moved to Hollywood: *Bill Bryson.*

3 *Wonder Bar*, the 1934 Warner Brother's film, not to be confused with *The Wonder Bar*, the 1931 stage show.

4 Frank Sinatra entered the Brunswick recording studio on Fifth Avenue for the first time in July 1939. His best work that summer was *All or Nothing at All,* an eventual hit and a number, which for a while, became a signature tune: *James Kaplan.*

5 Was Dr. Jekyll missing his Mr Hyde I wonder?

6 *Avalon*: This popular 1920 jazz standard was the subject of litigation between Puccini's publishers and the song's writers [Jolson; Buddy DeSylva and Vincent Rose]. It was claimed that the song's melody was based on melodic breaks in the aria *E Lucevan Le Stelle,* from the opera *Tosca.* The judge found in favour of Puccini, who was awarded $25,000 (equivalent to $ 320,000 in 2020) and all future royalties.

By Billy Merson - 1911 sheet music published by Jerome
Remick & Co. Via Public Domain
(Jolson's second million seller)

EPILOGUE

Having almost reached the end of my investigation into *Mister Jolson's* Broadway and early film career, also his association with the Afro-American idiom, I should now be in a position to answer my own question. Do I believe him to have been the world's greatest entertainer? Well, more about that shortly. During my excursion through the period under review, I discovered that this man had been many things. Not least a hit-maker. So much so that if you were a songwriter, and if he sang your song during this period, then you had a hit on your hands! He had been an established million-selling artist* before World War One. His success with, for example, the comedy number written by British music hall entertainer, Billy Merson, was to permeate the frozen wastes of Antarctica.

In the book, *Endurance*, by Alfred Lansing, about the 1914 explorations of Edwardian seaman, Ernest Shackleton, we read about how his crew of 28 spent their evenings, ice-bound for months in the Weddell Sea, staging concerts below deck to pass the time. In his diary, the ship's surgeon, Dr Maclin (in between amputating frost-bitten fingers and toes) managed to keep a detailed journal describing, among other things, how they blacked their faces and sang about the antics of *Spigoni* (The Spaniard that Blighted My Life and recorded by Al on March 7, 1913). It pleases me to tell you that the crew of the *Endurance* lived to tell their tale, proving that even when faced with such adversity, the spirit of man cannot be beaten. As for Mr

---
* Daily Mail Book of Golden Discs, Joseph Murrell (1966)

Frank Sinatra and Al Jolson 'talking shop', backstage at the Paramount Theatre, N.Y: Otis R. Lowe.

Jolson, his singing would continue to bolster the spirit of man - during two world wars and also the Korean conflict. Fast-forward now to 1946 and his morale-boosting efforts were acknowledged when a banquet was given in his honour by the Motion Picture Chapter of the American War Veterans Committee, at the Hotel Astor in New York. The proceedings were broadcast coast to coast. A galaxy of American vocal stars paid tribute by singing their own interpretations of 'Jolson Songs'. Most memorable for me is Frank Sinatra singing *Rockabye Your Baby with a Dixie Melody*, accompanied by Al's own conductor, Morris Stoloff. (It may still be available on YouTube).

> *What few people seem to grasp is that he [FS[is not simply the best popular singer of his generation, a latter-day Jolson or Crosby, but the culminating point in an evolutionary process which has refined the art of interpreting words set to music. Nor is there even the remotest possibility that he will have a successor. Sinatra was the result of a fusing of a set of historical circumstances which can never be repeated:*

Benny Green.

As for the Great American Songbook – it goes on. As of writing, Tony Bennett is still crooning. The late Nina Simone was a proponent and has left us some memorable albums. Michael Feinstein has been a revivalist, becoming friends and working with the legends Rosemary Clooney and Ira Gershwin. Canadian singer, Michael Bublé, with his boyish charm, built a career around the genre. Ageing rock star Sir Rod Stewart – who grew up listening to Jolson and Crosby (*vide: Rod Stewart: A Life on the Town, 1977*), collaborated with such as Cher and Queen Latifah, producing some marvellous tracks with amazing arrangements and backing, e.g.: *As Time Goes By,* also *Bewitched, Bothered and Bewildered.* Jazz, too, is still very much alive post millennium, although not easy to find on national radio (Jazz FM notwithstanding). One ensemble that is particularly worthy of note is Miss Elizabeth (Bougerol) and her *Hot Sardines.* Notable among their repertoire is: *Bei Mir Bist Du Schoen* [You are Beautiful]; *Running Wild* and *It Had to Be You,* the latter recorded at the Columbia Club, Indianapolis, USA in 2015. On this track the lovely Miss Elizabeth literally smoulders!

At the start of this Epilogue, I stated that Al Jolson had been many things. George Burns has told us that Al was a great comedian and also a fine monologist. In his BBC Radio 2 series – *I Call it Style* (1985), Hubert Gregg suggested that Jolson may have been peeved because, unlike George M. Cohan (who was an actor, composer, lyricist and playwright), he wasn't and this may have been the reason for the many 'cut-ins', where he insisted his name appear among writers credits. We debated this point, *via* the post, because there were instances where Al could have been included as a writer but chose not to be. One example, and cited by Wigransky in *Jolsonography,* is where he refused a hefty *payola* for adding his impetus to the song, Swanee. Al was not consistent, he could be downright contrary at times. As the composer and orchestra leader, Gordon *Lefty* Jenkins once said: 'You couldn't expect an artist of Jolson's calibre to be the same as the man who delivers your milk every morning'. Al Jolson referred to himself as a *song stylist,* rarely a singer, and as such probably believed this gave him licence to add (or dispense with) lyrics at will. This practice was only one of several devices that set the popular singer apart from his classical counterpart – who must deliver a composer's words as if they are a *holy writ.* Jolie took liberties with the lyrics of a song, in fact it is alleged he never did a number the same way twice. Sometimes this pleased the writers, sometimes it didn't. Frank Sinatra once incurred the displeasure of Cole Porter when, in performing *I Get a Kick Out of You*, he substituted *kick* with *boot.* It worked for Frank, but detracted from the aesthetics of the song – according to Porter who, during the early 1930s, had amended the lyrics himself to navigate around several sensitive issues of the time.[*]

Although perhaps more matador than troubadour, Jolson was innovative. He was the first to speak through the second verse and chorus of a song, a device known as the *patter bridge.* The best example of which, but not credited to Al, can be found in the 1926 ballad, *Are You Lonesome Tonight?* (Recorded on April 28th 1950 with the Gordon Jenkins Orchestra and Chorus).He was also the first to preface a song with autobiography, as in one performance of *Ma Blushin' Rosie* – "I was nothing. Just a poor little kid on the streets of Washington D.C. Shining shoes, selling papers or anything. . . ."

It had amazed me just how much the *post-mortem* Mister Jolson could affect people's lives (not least my own), something biographer, Michael Freedland called *The Jolson Touch.* At some point during the early 1970s when I worked as a ship draughtsman at Vicker's shipyard in Barrow-in-Furness, I was actively involved in union business – the Draughtsmen's & Allied Technician's Association. Our monthly periodical (*Tass*), occasionally contained articles by a Joe Ashton of Sheffield (who went on to be an MP). Mr Ashton was a no-nonsense kind of a guy, a straight-talker who struck me as being totally un-sentimental. On occasion I wrote to him in connection with union matters. Around fifteen years later (1985 or 86), Ashton had

---

[*] A reference to drugs (cocaine), also the kidnapping of Charles Lindbergh's baby son in 1932.

a weekly column in the *Daily Star* called Voice of the People in which he would champion the cause of the working man. On one occasion during the mid-eighties, when TV and Radio were marking the Jolson Centenary, Joe Ashton dedicated his entire column to the event. Accordingly I wrote to him. Upon reading his reply, it turned out that we had more in common than I had realised. Joe related how, in the late 1940s, if it hadn't been for Al Jolson he would still have been oiling and greasing steelworks plant in Sheffield! At that time he was an engineering apprentice attending a technical college in Rotherham. "From 1946 to 1950 Jolson was more popular than the Beatles and Elvis put together! The whole world seemed to go 'Jolson Crazy' because of two films about his life. Instead of brushing-up on my Bernoulli theorems and Venturi meters I was listening to Jolson records – and failed my exams! I owe my career in politics to Mr Jolson", Joe enthused.

I must end by again asking - Do I believe Al Jolson to have been the World's Greatest Entertainer? Firstly, perhaps 'believe' is not the right word to use. 'Belief' is an instinctive and emotional reaction to something beyond logic. A belief proves only the phenomenon of belief, not the content. Moreover, in considering the question I must revisit what Larry Adler told me right at the start of my investigation (1979) – "You had to see the man before a live audience", (Something I certainly never experienced). Accordingly I must be guided by those who had. And so who am I to cavil the words of, say, Pearl Sieben or Ralph Reader?

Al Jolson, by 1948 very much the elder statesman, with announcer, Ken Carpenter and warming-up prior to a Kraft Music Hall radio show: Otis R. Lowe.

Al Jolson, on a stage, either as himself or in the guise of Gus Jackson, was invincible. And there the matter rests.

APPENDIX

WHAT THEY HAVE SAID

'He needed applause the way a diabetic needs insulin. He was kind, sentimental and charitable to a fault. He was arrogant and surly. He was a braggart. He was crude and untutored. As a human being he left a lot to be desired. But he was the greatest entertainer the world has ever known' – **Mrs Pearl Sieben, Biographer**.

'You are arrogant if you think you are better than everyone else, Jolson knew he was the greatest, it was an absolutely assured knowledge' – **Larry Adler.**

'The father of popular singing in our time, Al taught us how to take care of the biz' – **Tony Bennett**.

I can't think of a luxury more attractive to me than having him with me for a while, I said for a while because he ate you alive, his energy ate you alive. **Irving Caesar, Lyricist.**

He had this incredible facility to make you believe what it was he was singing. **Sammy Cahn, Lyricist.**

What amazed me was that this great personality had never learned how to live. He couldn't; there was something chemically wrong. The minute the curtain rang down, he died. **Eddie Cantor, Entertainer.**

'I was once asked who were the great stage performers in my day, one who immediately comes to mind is Al Jolson, basically a silly man – let's do this, let's go there; let's go to the races - but in singing his ridiculous song, *Mammy,* by virtue of his stagecraft, he just elevated his audience and had them on the edge of their seats until he had finished' – **Sir Charles Chaplin.**

'He called himself the world's greatest entertainer, and he was, but with also the world's greatest ego' – **Saul Chaplin, arranger, lyricist.**

'When considering this man's talents one's thoughts turn naturally to superlatives, but somehow they seem inadequate' – **Bing Crosby.**

'No one funnier than *Mister*', **Kitty Doner.**

'Al was an inspiring performer – the embodiment of optimism who made one think the human soul could never be defeated'. **Herbert G. Goldman.**

Sometime during the late 1970s, during an episode of *Opportunity Knocks* on British television, host Hughie Green stated that he had once personally auditioned Al Jolson. Being sceptical, I wrote to Mr Green asking him to explain further. I wasn't too hopeful about getting a response but around two weeks later I received his reply, a hand written letter on personalised stationery. It transpired that Green was on his way to the U.S. from Deauville, France to meet- up with a record producer friend. 'Mr Jolson had agreed to try out a couple of songs for my friend in an empty theatre in Manhattan. So there it was', said Hughie, 'sat in this massive theatre with my friend and the great man singing just for us'. *(Hughie Green)*

I never liked him much, although he was a good singer – for that era. ***Harry Warren, Composer.***

TIN PAN ALLEY
A LANDMARK IN AMERICAN MUSIC

The measure of a song's success has always been gauged by its record sales. During the nineteen fifties the 12-inch, 78 rpm discs were still very much in vogue, but were slowly being superseded by the compact 7-inch, 45-rpm (mono) discs, which first appeared in 1949. These were known as *singles,* even though the record comprised two songs or tunes. The main title would be on what became known as the A-side, with a less popular number being on the B-side of the record. Years earlier, however, before the record player or phonograph became ubiquitous, popular music was issued on printed sheets called *sheet music* or score sheets, and as with discs, numbers of sales being a measure of success. *It is stated in the Introduction to this book that during the period discussed (1916 – 1931), there was no equivalent of today's mass popular music.* Gold and platinum discs are commonplace today but during the 20s, 30s and 40s, while there were 'million sellers', sales of 100,000 were considered hits!

Many of the early popular songs, that would comprise the Great American Songbook, were conceived in a 'song factory' known as Tin Pan Alley – the name originating, allegedly, from the cacophonous sound made by all the cheap and tinny upright pianos hammering out different tunes simultaneously. Tin Pan Alley was located in lower Manhattan on 28th Street between Sixth Avenue and Broadway and is estimated to have existed from

1890 until 1929. *(The 1945 Warner Brother's biopic of George Gershwin (Rhapsody in Blue), although largely fictional, contains a fairly accurate depiction of the Tin Pan Alley of 1919)*.

Slowly, music publishers moved onto 28th Street from other districts and by 1908 the place was firmly established. Over time the name came to represent the American music publishing business in general. An exceptional number of East European Jewish immigrants became the music publishers. Of these publishers, names like Willis Woodard; T.B. Harms and Jerome Remick were among the first to work in the 'popular' *genre.* Many of the men working in the 'music houses' had backgrounds as salesmen. For instance, a guy called Issi Witmark had peddled water filters, Leonard Feist had sold corsets and Joe Stern had sold neckties. Harry Cohn, who would later become the Iron Dictator of Columbia Pictures Corporation, started out as a song plugger, as did Irving Berlin, George Gershwin, Vincent Youmans and Harry Warren. During the early days of Tin Pan Alley copyright control was not so strict, publishers would often print their own versions of the songs popular at the time. Eventually, the situation regarding copyright was brought under stricter control and during 1914 the American Society of Composers, Authors and Publishers was founded. One of the biggest names at the time – George M. Cohan – was a principal driving force behind its establishment.

The start of Al Jolson's long career has been traced back to October 1900 when, as a boy soprano working with the tenor, Fred E. Moore, his name and likeness appeared on the cover of a published song by Charles K. Harris. Harris had written the Victorian ballad – *After the Ball* – and which became the bestselling song in the history of Tin Pan Alley (over 5 million copies sold).

By 1950 there were more than 5,000 song writers listed in the ASCAP Directory, the mind boggles when thinking what the figure is today.

A CRITICAL ANALYSIS: HENRY PLEASANTS

(This analysis, included here for the convenience of anyone wishing to delve deeper, also appeared in the centenary edition of the *Jolson Journal* (1985), as part of the feature – *Al Jolson Supervoice?* written by this author.

There was always in Jolson's singing characteristics distressing to the fastidious, whether of classical or jazz persuasion. His phrasing was blemished by habitual scooping and swooping, upwards and downwards, over intervals so wide that the effect was closer to wailing than singing. An agreeable but unexceptional voice, while skilfully used, was erratically focused, subject to abrasive nasality on such words as way, may, mine and time. His enunciation was extraordinarily distinct, but it was also appalling to those who treasured the King's English. He vitiated vowel sounds and tortured diphthongs. A word such as *you* for example might be pronounced as yoo, yew, yuh and you and all within the space of a few measures. Words of more than one syllable were methodically dismembered. The word melody for example, became mel-o-dee. Louis Armstrong always indulged in this device, and he may well have got it from Jolson.

His dynamics tended to be uniform, neither very loud nor very soft, and there was little variety of colour or timbre. He would seem to have been more concerned with the textual substance of a song than with its melodic contours. He was more orator than vocalist, a characteristic demonstrated again and again by his excursions into straight declamation. It was almost as if he found the tune inhibiting.

Therein lay the secret of his greatness. Therein, too, lay the root of his musical and linguistic misdemeanours. He loved words, and his maltreatment of them was a kind of smothering with affection. He would embrace a word, hug it, squeeze it, press it to his heart, and release it reluctantly the worse for wear. He often put more intensity into words than they could contain, or milked them for more than they could yield.

From none of this should it be inferred that he was unmusical. But as a musician he could find text and tune restrictive; hence the many whistling choruses, where he would break away from the tune and improvise and embellish, much as a jazz musician does. Sometimes he would throw in a few measures of vocalised imitation trombone. No. he was very musical. It was simply a matter of priorities, and he sorted them out according to his purposes. Like all singers he was better in some songs than others, and some songs suited him better than others. With conventional, sentimental ballads and with any kind of operetta-like material, he often sounded, early in his career, and before his voice began to darken, like a Jewish John McCormack. In later years he sometimes sounded like Bing Crosby who had begun by imitating him. The more conventionally he sang, the more conspicuous, the more dismaying, were his slurs, his nasality, his wayward treatment of vowels and diphthongs. He was always a strong performer with any song. But he would hardly be remembered today, or be reckoned a path breaker in popular singing, had he not hustled into Mammy's arms or followed the swallow back home.

It was in up-tempo coon songs that he was unique in his own time and prophetic of the future. Despite leaden rinky-tink instrumental backings, he could give a song tremendous bounce and drive. He was obviously trying to break away from the rhythmical strait-jacket of 1-2-3-4, to free syllables from their adherence to prescribed note values and lay them out in something closer to the rhythms of speech. In his 1929 recording of I'm Sitting on Top of the World, for example, he seems, briefly, to be distributing syllables at his own discretion over a four-measure span, achieving at least an approximation of the approach to phrasing advanced by Crosby and perfected by Sinatra. On the same record he also employs a Sinatra-like *rubato,* tarrying on 'top' and stealing from 'of the world'.

This performance, one of his best on record, is by no means an isolated example. In many of his early recordings you can hear him working towards the conversational rhythmic freedom and melodic cadences of the black vaudeville singers of the time. Personal reminiscences of Jolson in the early stages of his career include many references to his dropping into clubs in Chicago, New York and elsewhere to listen to black performers. It is impossible to sort out precisely what he picked up from them. One looks for clues in the records of those black artists only to find that they had been listening to Jolson just as intently as he to them.

It would be easy to assume that his slurring was derived from Negro example. Certainly he slurred for the same reason they did: to achieve something closer to rhetorical, oral communication than strict adherence to pitch would yield, and to heighten accentuation. But careful listening leads to the conclusion that his slurring was more cantoral, at least more Jewish, than Negroid. There was nothing contradictory or inconsistent in this. Eastern European Jew and Afro-American each had to make an accommodation to a Western European diatonic scale. Slurring was one way of getting beyond what the diatonic law would allow.

Others of Jolson's devices were obviously of black derivation. He liked to interpolate words and syllables, or repeat them, in the black gospel-song fashion, even throwing in the occasional 'Glory hallelujah' and 'Yessuh!' His frequent mauling of vowels may have been imitative, although his actual enunciation was not black. By the end of the 1920s, he was even indulging in jazzy 'boop-boop-a-doop' breaks.*

Pleasants, having delivered the above, objective, critique then goes on to almost dismiss it with the comment:- 'But given a live audience, he [Jolson] could always work the old magic'.

The late jazz critic, Benny Green, never a fan of Jolson's, was drawn to comment – "In the face of his many accomplishments, technical analysis is mere charlatanism'.

---

* I believe that Pleasants is referring to the 1930 Brunswick recording: When the Little Red Roses Get the Blues for You, (Joe Burke-Al Dubin). "Violets - send their regrets- when the little red roses get the blues for you, you, boop, boop-a-doop".

CELEBRITY CORRESPONDENTS

Adler, Larry. *Harmonica virtuoso.**

Ashton, Joe OBE, *British Politician, Author, Writer and Playwright.*

Bygraves, Max, OBE, *Entertainer.*

Fairbanks Jnr, Douglas. *Actor.**

Freedland, Michael. *Author, Broadcaster and Journalist.*

Green, Hughie. *Television Personality.* *

Gregg, Hubert, MBE, *Actor, Author; Broadcaster and Songwriter.*

Halliwell, Leslie. *Film Buyer, ITV and Channel 4; Author.*

Laine, Frankie. *Popular Singer; Dancer.**

Morley, Sheridan. *Actor, Biographer and Critic.*

Melley, George. *Jazz Singer, critic and writer.*

Reader, Ralph, CBE, *Choreographer, Songwriter.**

*Denotes those who had met and, or, seen Jolson perform.

BIBLIOGRAPHY

Works consulted in preparing this book:

Goldman, G Herbert. *JOLSON: The Legend Comes to Life,* (Oxford University Press, 1988). Ref.1

Pleasants, Henry. *The Great American Popular Singers,* (Simon and Schuster, 1974). Ref.2

Anderton, Barrie. *Sonny Boy: The World of Al Jolson,* (Jupiter Books Ltd, 1975).

Bryson, Bill. *One Summer in 1927,* (Doubleday, 2013).

Crosby, Bing & Martin, P. *Call Me Lucky,* 1953.

Freedland, Michael. *AL JOLSON,* (W. H. Allen, 1972).

Freedland, Michael. *Bing Crosby: the illustrated biography,* 1998.

Fisher, John. *Call Them Irreplaceable,* (Stein and Day, 1974).

Kaplan, James. *FRANK: The Making of a Legend,* 2012.

Potter, John. *Tenor: History of a Voice,* (Yale University Press, 2010).

Sieben, Pearl. *The Immortal Jolson,* 1962.

Wigransky, Dave. *Jolsonography,* (Barrie Anderton, 1969).

Papers and Periodicals:

The Jolson Journal, various issues, (International Al Jolson Society).

Jolson Poems, Ian Jones, 1977.

TV Times, various issues – 1977.

Websites:

www. broadwayworld.com

www.ibdb.com

www. jolson.org

www.playbill.com

Gus Kahn & Walter Donaldson / Public domain

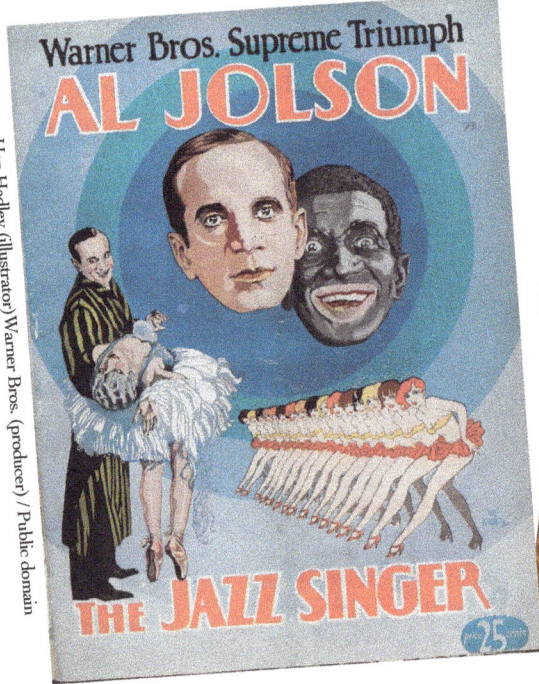

Hap Hadley (illustrator)/Warner Bros. (producer) / Public domain

United Artists / Public domain

The Heart of New York, originally issued as Hallelujah I'm a Bum (1933)

THE AUTHOR

Stan Henderson is a Barrovian Senior Citizen, born in 1949. His industrial life (30-years) was spent largely in the drawing offices of Vickers Armstrong (Shipbuilders) Ltd., (later VSEL), where he held a management grade senior staff position. For several years during the 1970s Stan was a part-time lecturer at Barrow College of Further Education. In 1995 he  took voluntary redundancy, leaving the shipyard to run a large convenience store with his sons on Walney Island. Since attaining retirement age he has co-authored two books on Barrow Steelworks. He has also penned a book about his shipyard apprenticeship as well as two local histories about Hindpool, Barrow-in-Furness. Stan now spends most of his time at a holiday home in Kirkby-in-Furness, South Lakeland.

Index

A

Abbott & Costello 46
About a Quarter to Nine 42
Abramson, Martin 11
Academy Awards 37
A Chazend'l Ohf Chabbes 43
Adler, Larry x, 53
After the Ball 58
Albertson, Chris 15
Algonquin Round Table 26
Al Jolson Society x, xii, 10, 22, 32, 65
Ambrose ix
American v, xii, 1, 11, 13, 14, 15, 19, 21, 22, 23, 24, 25, 27, 33, 46, 49, 50, 51, 57, 58, 61, 65
A Night in Spain 32, 33
April Showers 19
Are You Lonesome Tonight 52
Arlen, Harold v
Armstrong, Louis v, 13, 23, 59
Artists and Models 19, 27
ASCAP 25, 27, 58
Ashton, Joe 52, 53
Atlantic City 5, 33
Austin, Gene 31
Avalon 46, 47

B

Bailey, Mildred 23
Barton, James xi
BBC x, 13, 32, 37, 51
Beatles 53
Bechet, Sidney 23
Begin the Beguine 42
Beiderbecke, Bix 23
Bei Mir Bist Du Schoen 51
Benchley, Robert 26
Berkeley, Busby 42
Berlin, Irving v, 38, 58
Bernhardt, Sarah 46
Besserer, Eugenie 28
Big Boy 25, 26, 27, 29, 30, 35, 39, 42
Birth of a Nation 25
Black Actors Guild 12
blackface 1, 4
Blake, Eubie 11
Bombo 12, 17, 18, 19
Boston Opera House 11
Bougerol, Elizabeth 51
Boy Scout Gang Shows 19
Brice, Fanny 15
Broadway x, 1, 2, 3, 4, 5, 11, 19, 22, 36, 37, 43, 45, 46, 47, 49, 57
Brooklyn Eagle 44
Bryson, Bill 34
Bublé, Michael 51
Burbank Studio 39
Burns, George 8, 51

C

Caesar, Irving 22, 43, 46
Call Me Lucky 12, 15, 65
Calloway, Cab 23
Cantor, Eddie 17, 26, 29
Capone 29
Carson, Johnny 8
Caruso, Enrico 7, 8
Cats 3
Cellar, Edmond's 14
Chaliapin, Fyodor 46
Chaplin, Charlie 20, 21, 22, 30, 56
Cheek to Cheek 42
Cher 51
Clooney, Rosemary 51
Cohan, George M. 8, 51, 58
Cohn, Harry 58
Columbo, Russ 31
Columbus, Christopher 17
Connor, Edgar 22
Coogan, Jackie 21
Costello, Johnny 'Irish' 35
Cotton Club 12
Crewe, Regina 22
Crosby, Bing v, 12, 13, 15, 23, 25, 31, 41, 42, 47, 50, 51, 56, 60, 61, 65
Crosby, Harry Lillis (Bing) 12

D

Daily Star 53
Dancing in the Dark 42
Decca 32
DeForest, Lee 29
Dennis, Denny ix
DeSylva 33, 47
DeSylva, Brown and Henderson 33
Dodge Victory Hour 32
Doner, Kitty 2, 6
Don't Say Good-Night 42
Do what You Do 37
Dubin x
Dubin, Al 42
Dugan, Dixie 36

E

El Fey Club 35
Ellington, Duke 12
Elvis 53
Endurance 49
Entertainer, World's Greatest x
Epstein, Louis 46
Extravaganzas 25

F

Fairbanks, Douglas 21, 30
Fanny Brice 2, 15
Feinstein, Michael 51
Fields, Dorothy v
Fields, W. C. 21
Fisher, John xi

INDEX

Forty-Second Street 41
Frank, Perfectly xi
Freedland, Michael x, xiii, 19, 37, 46, 52
Fried, Martin 46
Frutti, Tutti v

G

Gable, Clark 5
Gaby DesLys 2
Garland, Judy 5
Gershwin v, 1, 22, 23, 25, 37, 42, 51, 58
Gershwin, George v, 22, 58
Gershwin, Ira 42, 51
Gest, Morris 43
Giddins, Gary 13
Girl, Show 36
Gold Diggers 41
Goldman, Herb xi, 27, 29
Goldman, Herbert 27, 41
Gone with the Wind 34
Good Evening, Friends 43
Goodman, Al 11
Gordon, Mack 42
Great American Songbook 1, 51, 57
Great Depression 39
Green, Benny xiii, 23, 32, 33, 47, 50, 62
Gregg, Hubert x, 42, 51
Griffith, D. W. 21, 25
Guaragna, Salvatore 42
Gus xi, xii, 1, 4, 9, 17, 21, 26, 39, 43, 53, 66

H

Hallelujah I'm a Bum 22
Hall, Mordaunt 22
Harlem 12, 14
Harris, Charles K. 58
Hart x
Henderson, Fletcher 'Smack' 15
Henderson, Stan 67
Hollywood 1, 21, 30, 33, 37, 42, 47
Home in Pasadena 23
Horse Exchange building 2
Hotel Astor 50
Hot Sardines 51

I

I'm Just Wild about Harry 11
In Old Kentucky 25
It Had to Be You v, 51

J

Jackson, Gus xi, 53
Jacobs, David x
Jenkins, Gordon 52
Jessel, Georgie 29
Jnr, Douglas Fairbanks 37
Jnr, Sammy Davies xi
Jolson, Al 1, i, v, vi, vii, ix, x, xi, xii, 1, 2, 3, 4, 5, 6, 7, 8, 9, 10, 11, 12, 13, 14, 15, 17, 18, 19, 21, 22, 23, 24, 25, 26, 27, 28, 29, 30, 31, 32, 33, 35, 37, 38, 39, 41, 42, 43, 44, 46, 47, 49, 50, 51, 52, 53, 55, 56, 58, 59, 61, 62, 63, 65
Jolsonaires x
Jolson Journal x, 59, 65
Joplin, Janis 15

K

Kapp, Jack 32
Karno, Fred 21
Keeler-Jolson, Ruby 41
Keeler, Ruby 35, 42
Kentucky Derby 26
Kern, Jerome v, 33
Kick Out of You 52
King of Jazz 23
Kit Kat Klub 44
Kraft Music Hall 24, 53
Kraft-Phoenix 24

L

Laine, Frankie xi
Lansing, Alfred 49
Latifah, Queen 51
Lauder, Harry 21
Lee, Dixie 41
Leroy's jazz club 12
Let Me Sing and I'm Happy 38, 39
Life magazine 26
Lindbergh, Charles 29, 52
Little Pal 36
Liza 37, 38
London Palladium 13
Looking at You 38

M

Ma Blushin' Rosie 52
Mae West 2, 46
Mammy ix, 9, 23, 25, 38, 56, 60
McAvoy, May 30, 31
McCarthy, Joe 5
McCormack, John 38, 60
Memories of You 15
Mercer, Johnny 42
Merson, Billy 49
Milestone, Lewis 46
Minnie the Moocher 23
Mister 6, 38, 49, 52, 56
Mister Bones 38
Monaco, James V. 5
Moore, Fred E. 58
My Mammy's Blues 23
My Sweetie Turned Sour on Me 23

INDEX

N
NBC 24
Netherland Apartment Hotel 35
New York Times 19, 22, 44
New York Winter Garden 2, 27
Night and Day 42
No, No, Nanette 22

O
Oh Donna Clara 43, 46
Old Man River 32
Oliver, King 23
Once in A While 42
Oscars 37

P
Pagliacci sketch 9
Parkinson, Michael 13
Parks, Larry xi
Perfectly Frank xi
Pickford, Mary 21
Pleasants, Henry xii, 13, 24
Poindexter 4
Pollard, Arthur 44
Porter, Cole x, 52
Potter, John 15
Prohibition 35, 44
Proust 11

R
Raphaelson, Samson 4, 44
Reader, Ralph 19, 25, 53
Rhapsody in Blue 23, 58
Richman, Harry 43
Ritz Tower 35, 43
RMS Berengaria 27
RMS Majestic 25, 27
RMS Mauretania 27
RMS Olympic 27, 35
RMSP Araguaya 27
RMS Umbria 27

Roaring Twenties vi, 39
Robinson Crusoe Jr 4, 5, 6, 9
Rodgers x
Rodgers and Hart x, 21
Romberg, Sigmund 17
Rose of Washington Square 37
Running Wild ix, 51
Ruth, Babe 29

S
Saint Louis Blues 23
Say it With Songs 37
Seldes, Gilbert xii
September in the Rain 42
Shackleton, Ernest 49
Show Boat 33, 47
Show Girl 36, 37
Shubert Brothers 2, 42
Shubert, Lee 42
Shubert Organisation 18
Shuffle Along 11
Sieben, Pearl 53
Silvers, Louis 19, 46
Simone, Nina 51
Sinatra, Frank v, 33, 47, 50, 52
Sinatra Music Society xi, xii
Sinbad 9, 11, 12
Sissle, Noble 11
Smith, Bessie 12, 13, 14
Smith, Whispering Jack 31
Society, Sinatra Music xi, xii
Sonny Boy ix, 33, 34, 37, 65
Spikes, Reb 23
SS Leviathan 27
Stage Door Canteen 44
Stardust v
Stella Mayhew 2
Stevenson, Robert Louis 11
Stewart, Rod 51
Stoloff, Morris 50
Sunday Night Concerts 17
Swanee 5, 9, 23, 37, 51
Swasey, William 2
swing era 14, 41, 42
Sylva, Buddy De 19

T
The Great American Popular Singers xii, 15, 24, 65
The Great American Songbook 1
The Jazz Age 22
The Jazz Singer i, x, 4, 23, 28, 29, 30, 33, 34, 37, 39
The New York Herald Tribune 41
There's a Rainbow 'Round My Shoulder 33
The Singing Fool 33, 34, 37
The Student Prince 18, 25
Theatre, Barrow's Coliseum 34
Theatre, Curran 46
Theatre, Four Cohans 33
Theatre, Imperial 17
Theatre, Jolson's 59th Street 17, 18, 25
Theatre, Nixon Apollo 5
Theatre, Nora Bayes 43
Theatre, Spokane's Auditorium 12
Theatre, Warner's 30
Theatre, Winter Garden 2, 17
Tilley, Vesta 2
Tin Pan Alley 1, 57, 58
Tonight's My Night with Baby 22
Trafalgar 35

U
United Artists 21, 46, 66

V
Vallee, Rudy 31
Venuti, Joe 23
Vitaphone Corporation 29
Vunderbar 43

INDEX

W

Waller, Thomas 'Fats' 12
Wall Street Crash 39
Warner Bros x, 28, 37, 66
Warner, Sam 30
Warren x
Warren, Harry 42, 58
Waters, Ethel v, 13, 15
Weber and Fields 43
Western Electric 29
When the Little Red Roses get the Blues for You 39
Where the Blue of the Night 31
White Christmas 31
Whiteman, Paul 23, 24, 32
Whiteman, Paul 'Pops' 23
Wigransky 51, 65
Winter Garden x, 2, 3, 4, 5, 9, 17, 18, 25, 27
Wonder Bar 42, 43, 44, 45, 46, 47
World's Greatest Entertainer x, 53

Y

Yoelson 1, 27
You Are Too Beautiful 42
Youmans, Vincent 58

Z

Zanuck, Daryl 30
Ziegfeld, Flo 37
Ziegfeld Follies 26, 27

ALSO BY THE SAME AUTHOR

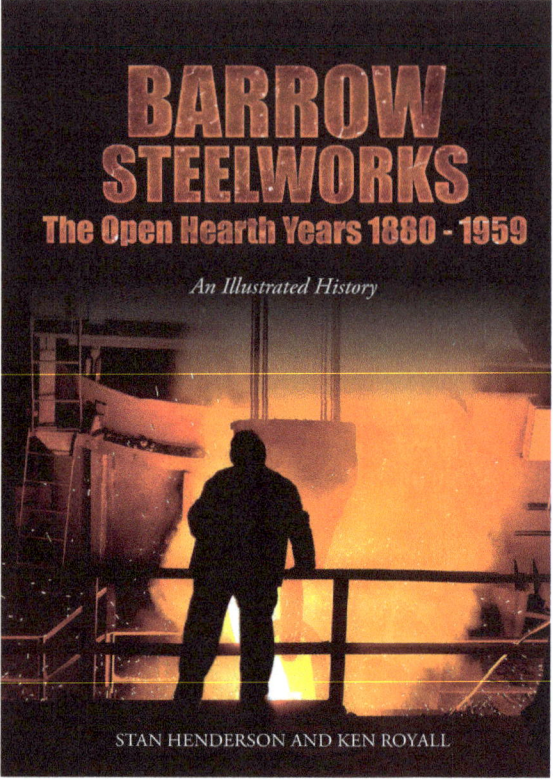

During the second half of the nineteenth century, Barrow-in-Furness became a pioneer in iron and steel production. It went on to grow astronomically – owning collieries in three counties and ore mines in two – and became the largest integrated steelworks in north Lancashire and Cumberland and, at one time, the largest steelworks in the world. Its success was due, in part, to having the prestige of three dukes as directors, as well as to being only 2 miles away from one of the largest and richest iron ore mines in the country.

The 1880s were a decade of change for Barrow works with some of the main players departing the scene. The arrival of the basic method of steelmaking, took away the lucrative position held by the directors and shareholders who had drained the coffers leaving virtually nothing for re-investment. After the Great War the company was limping along. The evacuation of Dunkirk at the start of WWII together with the blocking of special steels produced a demand for the kind of steel the making of which Barrow was a past master. Under United Steel's banner Barrow would see security of employment.

available at
amazon

available at
amazon

Paperback: 160 pages
Publisher: The History Press;
Language: English
ISBN-13: 978-0750963787

Paperback: 98 pages
Publisher: Stanley Henderson
Language: English
ISBN-13: 978-0995619050

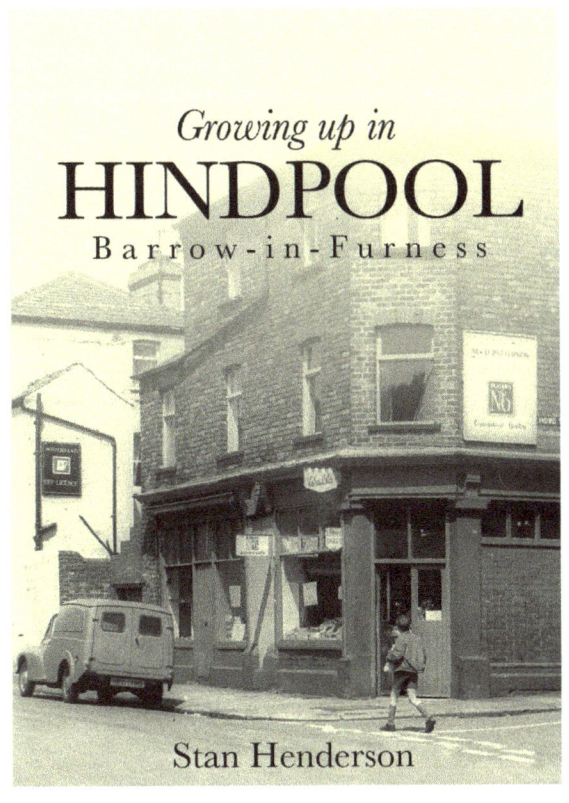

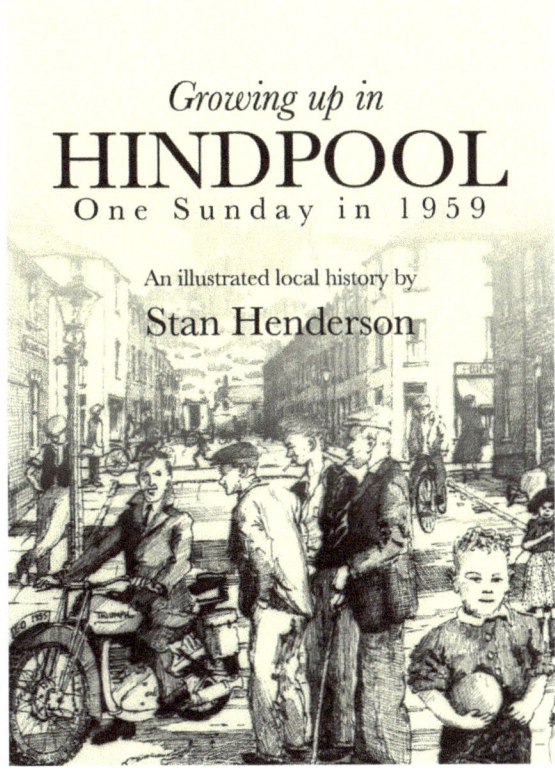

The history of Hindpool has been likened to a patchwork quilt, with each fragment, or patch, different in time, size, shape and colour. In his book the author has woven his quilt with the thread of family history and personal experience. The story starts with the arrival in Barrow of the writer's ancestors, immigrants from Shropshire, who had come to work on the blast furnaces of the local, monster, Ironworks. These works would later hold an unexplained fascination for the author, who, in this book takes the reader on a conducted tour around the historic works.

In this follow-up to Growing Up in Hindpool, the author completes his patchwork quilt with respect to the industries, institutions and businesses to which he has been directly or indirectly involved. The reader is taken on a walk out of the district and, via Lower Cocken, into Ormsgill, then back into Hindpool. During this walk, which 60-years ago, was undertaken at least once per week, the author reflects upon aspects of 1950's life, bygone industries, landmarks and some of the local characters that made Hindpool one of Barrow's most fascinating places in which to belong.

available at

available at

Paperback: 140 pages
Publisher: Stanley Henderson
Language: English
ISBN-13: 978-1916021747

Paperback: 84 pages
Publisher: Stanley Henderson
Language: English
ISBN-13: 978-1916275836

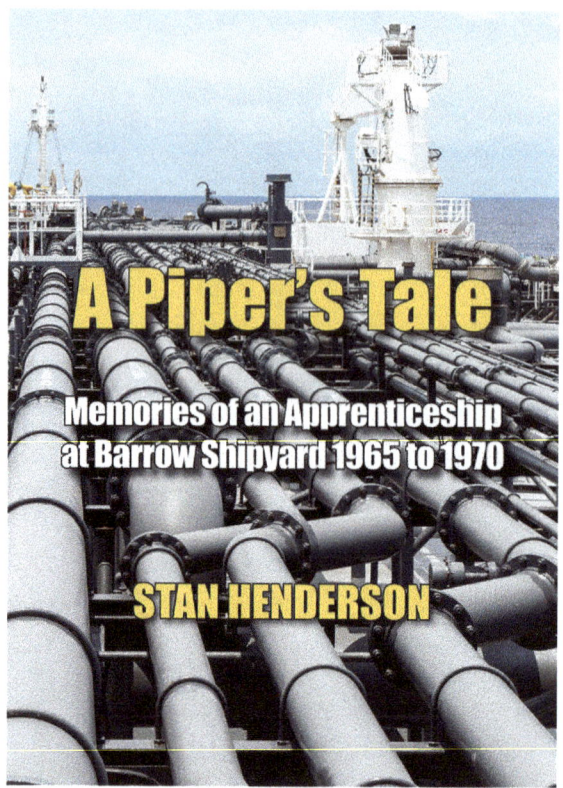

A Pipers Tale records the impressions made on a teenager as he makes his way into the thorny world of shipbuilding. A world in which the author, during the 1960s, witnessed the change from traditional shipbuilding, where vessels were constructed with a minimum, but adequate, level of technical support via long established trade practices and skills, to the cutting-edge of science-based projects as the Yard at Barrow became a 'Leader in Marine Technology' with the making of sophisticated warships and first-of-class vessels. Saluting the the wealth of characters and personalities that comprised the Yard's Plumbing Fraternity.

Paperback: 96 pages
Publisher: Stanley Henderson
Language: English
ISBN-13: 978-0995619081